THE CLEVER CONNECTOR

The Easiest Way to Become Powerful, Regardless of Your Situation.

The Underdog's Guide to Networking with Billionaires, Celebrities, and Executives

ALI SCARLETT

FOREWORD BY LUCIO BUFFALMANO

The Clever Connector © Copyright <<2020>> Ali Scarlett

All rights reserved. No part of this publication may be reproduced, distributed or transmitted in any form or by any means, including photocopying, recording, or other electronic or mechanical methods, without the prior written permission of the publisher, except in the case of brief quotations embodied in critical reviews and certain other noncommercial uses permitted by copyright law.

Although the author and publisher have made every effort to ensure that the information in this book was correct at press time, the author and publisher do not assume and hereby disclaim any liability to any party for any loss, damage, or disruption caused by errors or omissions, whether such errors or omissions result from negligence, accident, or any other cause.

Adherence to all applicable laws and regulations, including international, federal, state and local governing professional licensing, business practices, advertising, and all other aspects of doing business in the US, Canada or any other jurisdiction is the sole responsibility of the reader and consumer.

Neither the author nor the publisher assumes any responsibility or liability whatsoever on behalf of the consumer or reader of this material. Any perceived slight of any individual or organization is purely unintentional.

The resources in this book are provided for informational purposes only and should not be used to replace the specialized training and professional judgment of a health care or mental health care professional.

Neither the author nor the publisher can be held responsible for the use of the information provided within this book. Please always consult a trained professional before making any decision regarding treatment of yourself or others.

For more information, email info@aliscarlett-author.com.

ISBN: 978-0-578-71414-1

GET YOUR FREE GIFT!

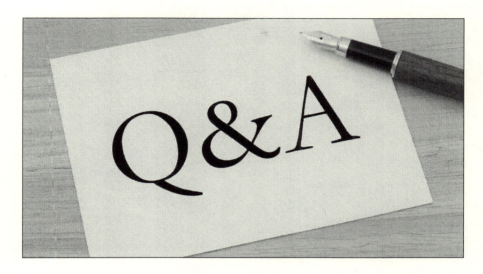

To get the best experience with this book, I've found readers who join our mailing list and use their free Q&A chat session with the author are able to implement faster and take the next steps needed to achieve their goals.

You can get your free Q&A chat session with the author by visiting: www.thecleverconnector.com/freegift

Dedication

I would like to dedicate this book to the following people:

This book is dedicated to my father, who was willing to accept his faults and learn from them in order to develop as a man and improve into becoming the best father a son like me could ask for. For being an inspiration for my own personal self-development, this book is dedicated to you.

This book is also dedicated to my high school teacher, Jeremy G. Johnson. More than the best school teacher I've ever had, but a good friend and a great man. For showing me the kindness I deeply needed when I was facing hardship, this book is dedicated to you.

Table of Contents

Foreword ix

Introduction xv

Step One: *Know the Power Dynamics* 1

Step Two: *Adopt the Helpful Mindsets* 19

Step Three: *Remember the Basic Rules and Principles* 51

Step Four: *Networking Strategies to Connect* 67

Step Five: *Get a Mentor. Then, Get Another One.* 95

Step Six: *Make Your Own Opportunities* 107

Next Steps 117

Epilogue: *This Is Not the End. Quite the Opposite.* 119

Acknowledgments 127

Notes 131

About the Author 141

Foreword

Ali Scarlett and I have crossed paths online on numerous occasions, recently connected more formally, and I look forward to eventually meeting him in person.

Yes, we have not yet met in person. And yet… It feels like Ali is an old friend.

When I first encountered Ali, he reminded me of a scene from *The Dreamers*.

The Dreamers is a movie about movie buffs whose lives revolve around movies. The protagonist calls himself one of the "insatiables." These are the guys who can never have enough, the type of guys who sit as close as possible to the screen so they can receive the images first.

Ali seemed to have that same spirit. But instead of movies, it was personal development, growth, and strategies for success. He was one of the insatiables, asking the most questions, reading the most books and always working the hardest.

What a winner.

Incidentally, this is what I love about networking in the digital age we live in.

Your potential is not bound by the physical world anymore. The information, the teachers, and the people available to you today can truly give you wings and make you free, *no matter your past and regardless of your current station in life*. It doesn't matter if you're in what Trump would have called a shit-hole country, a God-forgotten village of farmers (like where I grew up), with an abusive parent (like Ali had), or if, at a certain point in life, you were desperate and couldn't see a light at the end of the tunnel (like both Ali and I have been).

Somewhere out there, there is someone who can help you stand back up and show you the way to a level of success that you could have never dreamed of.

I don't know your current station in life. Maybe you are having difficulties seeing the light at the end of the tunnel.

Or maybe you're well outside that tunnel, but you are one of the "insatiables" driven to have more, be more, and do more in your life.

Or maybe you just want something better for yourself. In any case, this book will help you.

But before you plunge in, a quick heads up: the power of your network is potentially limitless. But, as Ali will explain, networking is an exchange. This means that the only limits to who you want to network with, learn from, and work with are your personal drive, your skills as a networker, and the value you bring to the table.

People skills are *crucial* in this world.

Right now, I am living a digital nomad lifestyle, doing exactly what I love doing and living exactly the life of freedom I dreamed of living. People and networking have been crucial to getting where I am right now.

Yet, there was a time not long ago when I was as clueless as the next guy when it comes to people, networking strategies, and psychology.

I still remember when I first learned the power of networking, relationships, and general soft skills (which I now refer to as "executive skills"). I was in my graduate talent program, interviewing to get into the big restructuring project that had just started.

McKinsey was launching the program for us. It was a colossal opportunity to network with the upper management and learn from the most driven consultants—always get into any restructuring projects if you can.

That day, Michael, an IT SVP, was interviewing in the teleconference room. He asked me why I wanted to join the program. Working with the little I knew, I said I wanted to join so I could "learn the lean methodology."

His answer was a tectonic shift at how I looked at personal development and career growth. He said, "Are you here to learn the lean methodology, or to learn about people skills? The methodology is useful, but an even bigger opportunity is to learn soft skills. Things like leadership, persuasion, presentations..."

Yep. I went in there focusing on technical skills, but Michael Schlitt (I still remember his name) showed me that the methodology—the technical skills—meant little to those who had real power. He even did it without making me feel like an idiot for my answer. He showed me, with a brimming smile, what being an SVP was all about—and it wasn't about technical skills. Michael didn't know shit about lean methodology.

Power is all about people skills, soft skills—what I now call "executive skills." The executive skills—which Michael didn't mention, because those are part of the "unspoken skills"—also included knowledge and mastery of power dynamics. It included things like speaking with confidence, looking authoritative, and knowing who to ally with.

His answer had left me speechless. It was that day I realized: tech skills give you job security. People skills give you board seats.

It's all too common that we see younger folks focusing solely on developing their hard skills in an attempt to make more money and achieve their goals quicker, but life satisfaction rarely comes from money or getting a "good job." This book will teach you how to leverage an even more fundamental form of power that will make you not just more successful, but far happier and fulfilled. At the end of the day, only other people can give you happiness and fulfillment.

As Brene Brown said, "Connection [with other humans] is why we're here."

Oh, P.S.:

Ali insisted that I write something about me.

I hold a master's degree from La Sapienza, department of communication and sociological research, and I am a member of the American Psychology Association (APA).

My mission is to empower underdogs with knowledge of the unwritten rules of the world—things such as life strategies, psychology, persuasion, and anything related to people and social dynamics.

I believe that without that knowledge, good people and underdogs alike will always be screwed by the ones who are born rich, ruthless, or less conscientious (or all of them). Learning power dynamics and effective people strategies is the only way to level the playing field.

That's what I love about Ali's work: he was not blessed with a silver spoon in his life. He had to carve his way up, and he used people skills to do it.

This book will help you, too, carve your way up. It will empower you with the knowledge, tools, and resources you need to do your best with those who matter the most to your success: other people.

Are you thinking you don't need this? That's exactly what all the average folks think—and no offense to average folks, truly.

In my work and in my life, I see an endless stream of people who are killing their chances because of silly, people-related blunders.

They screw themselves up by breaking the basic, unwritten rules of social interactions.

They ruin a relationship with unneeded confrontational frames, they inadvertently offend superiors, or they simply fail to come across as people worth networking with (and that includes people who *are* worth networking with).

Most of the time, those mistakes were avoidable. If they had only known the very basics of people and success strategies...

While those painful experiences *can* serve as great teachers, not everyone learns from them. This book will help you understand those unwritten rules so you will not make those silly mistakes in the first place.

You will instead start doing what works.

Ali has screened each strategy and technique for its effectiveness, drawing from some of the best authors around. This book is well-referenced, practically-oriented, and real-world tested, which is exactly the approach I love and use in my own work.

What makes Ali's book so unique is the perfect combination of high-quality writing, top-notch strategies, and his own highly inspirational story.

Foreword

Read it, internalize it, exercise it. I am confident that this book will be a big stepping stone in your road to success, personal empowerment, and life satisfaction.

To you, my friend, and to your continued success.

Lucio Buffalmano
Founder, ThePowerMoves.com

Introduction

I decided to write this book because I suffered from depression and suicidal thoughts as a child. Back then, I always felt like no one cared about me, which made me feel alone in the world. I felt like I couldn't understand what my purpose for being alive was, if I had to live in isolation. Anytime I would learn about money, I'd make believe I had all the expensive luxuries I wanted. I felt like the people in my life would *have* to care more about me if I had a lot of status or wealth. I set ambitious goals for myself and, even though I didn't have people I could count on in my life, I had goals I could fight for in my life. Goals that helped me feel happier on my own because I finally felt like I had a purpose in the world!

People often experience things in life that force them to choose between giving in to life's strain or fighting through to the other side. They set goals for themself that help them overcome those bitter experiences and fight with everything they have for those goals. They refuse to give in to the awful circumstances that life throws at them. I want to reach those people and inspire them to continue fighting for their goals. I want to give them the tools they need to stay the course so they can avoid falling into the self-destructive habits I found myself in. The negative habits that developed when I let the unfairness of life beat me, mentally and emotionally. That is why I committed myself to creating this book.

My belief that wealth and status was the answer to the problems within my social life led me to become deeply immersed in my research of money and power. I was constantly reading, scanning, studying, and taking notes on hundreds of articles, books, journal entries, essays, and reports in all things related to money, personal finance, self-development, and self-help.

Growing up, I always thought that money was, simply, power, and that was that. It was only the rich who had the power to get away with murder (both figuratively and literally), only the rich who could afford the luxurious lifestyle that people were jealous of, and only the rich who people really had an incentive to care about, since they had so much, well, power.

However, throughout my research, my own painful experience, and the pain I had seen others experience, I found myself calling into question how I viewed power.

I began to feel that the world was relying too much on money as a form of power. As a result, they were suffering from the numerous opportunities that were slipping through their fingers. Opportunities they couldn't even see.

I soon realized that my lack of money was not the problem; it was only a *result* of the problem. The popular literature on attaining wealth only addressed the symptoms, leaving the underlying chronic problems untouched. This would explain why money is still such a big issue for so many in today's world.

In addition to my research of self-development and money, I began to delve into the art of networking. I even went so far as to take a Yale University course in negotiation and persuasion. I performed field testing to discover which persuasion strategies work in ethically persuading others to join my network and which don't. By working on my networking skills and learning power dynamics, I became better at communicating, developed a more wholesome personality than the cold one caused by my depression, and built healthy relationships with people who helped me advance to life's next levels (and I didn't need tons of money to do it).

Young professionals, college students, and many others who used to struggle to progress toward their goals without the aid of a robust network have already experienced great success by implementing the tips, tricks, and strategies found in this helpful how-to guide.

The strategies I will be sharing with you in this book have created strong business relationships, attracted millionaire investors, and launched brand-new, successful careers. By the end of this book, I promise that you will have the "aha moment" that will set you apart. If you apply the concepts correctly, you will be able to achieve any goal

Introduction

you set for yourself in your personal life and career. These strategies and networking secrets will give rise to exclusive opportunities for your career, regardless of what industry you're in.

Now, this book is not for people who think they already know everything they need to know about networking. People with that mindset will approach the strategies and information laid out inside this book with a closed mind and won't be able to see the maximum benefits. As an acquaintance of mine would often say, "Our mind is like an umbrella; it only works if it's open." This book is also not for people who have a fixed mindset and no desire to change that mindset.

"In a fixed mindset, people believe their basic qualities, like their intelligence or talent, are simply fixed traits. They spend their time documenting their intelligence or talent instead of developing them. They also believe that talent alone creates success—without effort."**[1]**

In other words, if you don't believe you can develop the abilities that will take you to the next level, there's no sense in you reading this book. It would be a waste of your time. If you currently have a fixed mindset and aren't willing to change your perspective—if you aren't willing to decide that yes, you can improve your skills in the areas necessary to advance your career and get more out of life—then, once again, this book isn't for you.

Anyone who has a growth mindset or is willing to switch to one to become better, please know that waiting to read this book will cost you in the long run. Avoid being the person who misses out on opportunities in life because you hesitated to apply the strategies outlined in this book. Be the kind of person other people marvel at. Be the kind of person other people see and say, "I don't know how they do it."

Relationships are essential to your success, as well as to the achievement of your goals. You must build the relationships you need before you need them. You must network now, or you'll be kicking yourself later! I hope you're excited to learn the most effective networking strategies to develop your personal power, advance your career, better connect with others, and become a better you. The networking tips and tricks you're about to read have been proven to create positive, long-lasting results. All you have to do to develop your

THE CLEVER CONNECTOR

dream network is to keep reading. Each chapter will give you new insight as you strive to establish a robust web of powerful connections. Take control of your life right now, use the powerful strategies you're about to learn responsibly, and enjoy the new life you're creating.

Step One

Know the Power Dynamics

Growing up, I was something of a "nice guy." I was always treating others how I would want to be treated to the maximum capacity. As a kid, there were days in school when I would catch someone sneaking a peek at my paper during a test. Torn between a rock and a hard place, I would ask myself, "If I needed to get the right answers on a test from someone else, would I want them to help me?" The answer was yes. Sometimes I would even secretly slide my paper closer to the student cheating off my paper, so they could get a better look. I was that guy. I was raised with values that encouraged my behavior to be like this all the time.

There was a day when I was around seven years old that I had gotten forty dollars for Christmas. Later that day, while running some errands, I noticed a man from the Salvation Army ringing a bell. He had a red bucket beside a sign asking for donations. Without a second thought, I dropped all my money in the bucket—then watched in confusion as my mother shuffled through the man's bucket to get some of the money back. I had done what I had been raised to do: treat others the way I wanted to be treated. I knew that if I were that man, possibly freezing out in the cold, working to gather donations for a noble cause, I would have wanted that forty dollar donation. So, I gave it to him. I was raised with values that encouraged my behavior to be like this all the time.

My mother never fully explained her reasoning behind taking some of the money back. It wasn't often that I saw her contradicting the values she helped to raise me with, so I trusted her judgment and brushed it off as a "one time thing." By brushing it off, I continued to treat others the way I wanted to be treated and carried out that value to its fullest extent.

These nice guy habits of mine almost always worked against me, but it wasn't until I got older that I really started to notice that pattern. As I neared adulthood, I began to see that people were taking advantage of me. I maintained my kindness, because I was happy so long as I was doing what I believed was right—but as my friends started to act less like friends while still taking from me, I began to rethink the extent to which I should carry out the values I was raised with.

I could feel people distancing themselves from me and caring less about my well-being. In an effort to be more accepted in my social circles and to feel less isolated, I started cracking more jokes and developed a funnier personality. When I was around, people liked me because I was a funny guy. However, when I wasn't around, no one seemed to care. No one checked in on me to see if I was doing okay. When I did get the chance to talk to someone over the phone, the conversation was focused on them. The funny thing about that is that a large part of me actually preferred it that way. When I wasn't around and they didn't reach out to me, I rationalized that it was okay because that meant more time for me to focus on my schoolwork. When we did get the chance to talk over the phone and they were talking about themselves, it was usually about some sort of drama they were experiencing in school and I saw this as an opportunity to help them. I knew that if I were in their shoes experiencing that drama and was in need of advice, I would want that help.

Then, there came a day when I was hospitalized after having my first near-death experience. I had just been diagnosed with kidney failure and had no idea what was happening to me. As I woke up from the large doses of morphine and oxycontin, my eyes opening slowly, I quickly grabbed my phone, gripping it tightly as waves of pain surged through my body. I eagerly checked if anyone had texted me but found that there were no new messages. Disappointed, I found myself in a world of confusion. I had been out of school for weeks fighting this illness. When I collapsed and was rushed to the hospital, laying on what could have easily been my death bed, I expected at least one of my friends to have reached out to me, since they had not seen me in so long. There was not one text, no missed calls, and seemingly no care at all from their side.

As grim as this experience may sound, luckily, another one of my values is not to judge someone else's choices when you don't understand their reasons. So, stupidly, I rationalized to myself that perhaps none of their phones were working. I remained hopeful as I scanned their social media to search for answers as to why they had forgotten to check on my well-being. Immediately, I understood. Their social media accounts were filled with pictures of them having a good time at parties and on my soccer team. I saw them enjoying themselves at the school basketball games and playing video games at their friend's houses. The only exceptions were a couple of posts that read, "Bored. Hit me up."

Naturally, I was angry. I had nearly died, and nobody cared.

That day, I went from being a "nice guy" to being a bully. At the time, my number one need was acceptance, and it seemed like no matter what I did, I couldn't get it. I was already being abused at home by my family, so my friends were all I had—and now it seemed like I didn't have them either.

In the following weeks, people began to distance themselves from me without caring if I noticed. Even good guys have bad days, but they could immediately tell something deep inside me had changed. I was willing to hurt anyone, because I didn't care about my own life anymore.

I was hoping someone would see the emotional pain I was in and care about me for once. I was hoping someone would see the anger inside my heart and be able to empathize with me. I was hoping that the person who understood me wouldn't judge me for who I'd become, because they'd understand how I felt inside. I was hoping that they wouldn't judge my choices because they would understand my reasons. I was hoping that others would treat me the way I would want to be treated.

I couldn't understand how it could be that I was a good person before and was alone, and now I was a bad person and was still alone. I had drawn the conclusion that the people I had called my "friends" were always fake, and that my sickness was all they needed to take their masks off. I was depressed, suicidal, and couldn't have cared less about whether I lived or died.

Eventually, I had to face the fact that I didn't have it in me to commit suicide. I wished I did because to me that would have been the equivalent of a shortcut to heaven. Back then, I felt like life was a prison. You're not given a choice to be born in the world, but it's illegal to try to suicide your way out. You don't have a choice but to wake up and deal with all the cruel experiences life throws at you on a regular basis. You're stuck here until your time comes.

It was only after I realized that I wasn't ever actually going to commit suicide that I started to work on myself and see things a different way. I created goals for myself that forced me to improve, and I took steps outside of my unenthusiastic mindset.

I eventually started to feel like death would have been the real prison. Since I'm alive, I still have the choice to either kill myself or do something with my life. When I'm dead, there's no choice. There's no freedom. When you're alive, you have the option of death—but when you're dead, there is no option of life. That realization was the wake-up call I needed to start working harder on my goals. Luckily, my goals no longer involved death.

At the time, my ultimate goal was to make everyone feel bad for isolating me by getting rich. I knew that I needed a "socially impressive" achievement in order to gain their respect. In other words, I knew they'd care more about me if I pulled up to school in a sports car. It wasn't the most noble reason to go after my goals, but it kept me moving forward. With a little more spring in my step, I started to research money. I needed to get closer to my goals, and I needed money to do it.

I believed money was power. Later, I was taught that there are actually three forms of power in the world: resources, information, and weaponry. We all know how money works as power, and we can all look back to the last world wars to know how weaponry works as power, but the idea that information could be a form of power was cheesy to me. It felt like an attempt to sell me the idea that "knowledge is power." Then, I saw the examples. The way information was used as blackmail to gain power over other people. The way information was used to make more money than the next guy in the stock market.

The "knowledge is power" concept was still cheesy to me at the time, so I didn't take it too seriously back then, but the examples were interesting. Out of curiosity, I started to dig more into the idea of power and what it really was. That was when I discovered power dynamics, and everything began to make sense.

Power dynamics, at its most simplistic, is the way in which power works in a setting. Power is the measure to which an individual can get what he wants. The word "dynamic" is synonymous with the word "process." To that end, "power dynamics" is the process by which a person can get what he wants in a given setting.

My research of power dynamics taught me that power infuses all relationships. For example:

"In social psychology, the stereotype content model (SCM) is a model, first proposed in 2002, postulating that all group stereotypes and interpersonal impressions form along two dimensions: (1) warmth and (2) competence."**[1]**[1]

In other words, the stereotype content model suggests that groups and individuals assess each other along two dimensions:

1. **Warmth**: is he friend or foe?

2. **Power**: how powerful is he?

"The original research refers to 'competence' instead of power.**[2]** But since 'competence' is defined as 'the capacity to enact one's intentions'**[3]**, that's basically also the definition of power."

"The two axes form four quadrants. See it below with examples for each quadrant on the categories (1) politics, (2) work, and (3) relationships"**[4]**:

---

[1] Information and graph regarding the stereotype content model provided by power dynamics expert Lucio Buffalmano. See Notes section for more.

	Low Power	**High Power**
High Warmth	• King's servant • Clueless intern • Nice beta provider • The person nobody cares about	• Beloved king • High EQ founder & leader • Women's dream man • The person everyone wants to be around
Low Warmth	• Deposed despot • Frustrated civil servant • Jealous cuckold • The person everyone loves to hate	• Hated dictator • "Stay-away type" CEO • Abusive husband • The person nobody wants to cross

With this fascinating research, it all made sense why no one seemed to care about me. Even as a kid, I knew that if I was a multimillionaire or celebrity people would immediately start to care about me, even though I would have been a human being before and after acquiring that wealth or status.

When I was a nice guy, I had high warmth but low power. I had high warmth because I was always willing to give. But, by being willing to give everything to anyone, everyone felt like they had power over me and therefore saw me as low-power (cracking so many jokes for group acceptance didn't help their image of my worth, either).

"For most non-powerful people, submission and high-warmth are signals to avoid confrontations. So we tend to associate very high levels of friendliness and submission with low-power."[5] So, in my relationships, I was the person nobody cares about. The overly-friendly nice guy who finished last.

When I became frustrated and turned into a bully, I was high-power. I was capable of harming anyone with no regrets about the consequences, since I didn't care about my own life. My aggression made me low-warmth. I became the person nobody wants to cross, and intimidated people into distancing themselves from me because of it.

Know the Power Dynamics

Basically, I failed the social test created by the unwritten rules of social interactions. When I came to this realization, it was one of the biggest "Aha!" moments of my life.

I was able to clearly see the powerful impact of power dynamics in my social interactions (and social life as a whole). I saw, with total clarity, the conflicts between what I thought to be true based on the values I was taught as a child and the honest, true-to-life power dynamics that I was surrounded by, day in and day out.

I also learned that if your bracket changes, people also change their attitudes toward you. If you are high-power and high-warmth now, it's unrealistic to think that if you suddenly become low-power everyone will still want to be around you. For example, if you were once a well-known celebrity but that is no longer the case, you can't expect everyone to want a picture with you. You became low-power, so the attitudes of others changed.

Some of my high school classmates were high-warmth and considered high-power solely because they had a car, which was not common in these circles but highly desirable. One particular guy became low-power after his car broke down. People would still talk to him, but mainly to check if his car had been fixed yet. When his car was repaired, people began talking to him normally again as well as asking him for rides.

High school is a pretty judgemental environment and is different from college and the real world, so you may not run into situations as extreme as that, but the same dynamic occurs in life outside of school every day.

The highest bracket was clearly the high-warmth, high-power one in the top right. But I also understood that when you achieve that high-power and high-warmth bracket, just because everyone wants to be around you doesn't mean it's because everyone genuinely likes you. Your high-warmth personality and high-power success attract people like a magnet. Some of the people you attract will be haters, or even gold-diggers.

Be that as it may, that doesn't change the "celebrity effect" high-power, high-warmth people have. That celebrity effect would open doors of opportunity that I wouldn't be able to open in any other bracket.

As I continued my research, I saw opportunities to apply my newfound knowledge of power dynamics to the achievement of my goals. If I could become high-power and high-warmth, I could be the person everyone wants to be around. I could fix my social life.

I knew I could work on myself and become high-warmth again, but this time in a way that was more sensible, healthy, and self-respectful. I understood that I could create my own experience: if I looked and acted like an unapproachable bully, I would be treated like an unapproachable bully. So, all I had to do was to go back to liking people. Okay, cool. I can do that.

Becoming high-warmth again was easy. The real question was how to become high-power.

I concluded that I had to become high-value to become high-power. High-value means exactly what it sounds like: you have a high amount of value. You could have a high amount of value in terms of your looks, your status, your resources (lots of money and lots of powerful connections), etc. If I gained a lot of value in certain areas, I could become high-power and mix it with high-warmth to achieve the best bracket of the SCM mix. My plan was to start with acquiring value in the form of money, and then use that money to acquire status.

While that's certainly one way to go, I drew the conclusion that this was the right course of action much too soon. I learned one simple rule that changed everything for me.

I learned that perceptions are reality[6]. To better illustrate this rule, let's take an example. Let's say you're walking down the street and see a woman sitting down on a bench while waiting for her ride. You notice that she's wearing a wedding ring on the ring finger of her left hand. Most would assume she's married, but does that necessarily mean that's the reality? Does her wearing a wedding ring guarantee that she's married? There are plenty of attractive, unmarried women who wear wedding rings to keep from being approached by men throughout their day.

Know the Power Dynamics

In another example, take the videos of millionaires "going undercover," posing as homeless people as part of a social experiment. They were perceived as homeless people and were definitely treated like it. The perceptions became the reality, despite the truth being that they were well-off financially.

In other words, even if I only developed the *traits* of a high-value man, if I looked and acted the part, I would be perceived as one. This would be true even if I wasn't actually high-value yet (in the sense that I wasn't a billionaire). I would be what is referred to as a "high-quality man" in power dynamics.

A high-quality man is a man with the traits that directly affect their personality (in a positive way) or, more or less indirectly, allow the individual to acquire important life assets such as status, resources, mates, or friends. These are the traits of a high-quality man[7][2]:

1. He is Emotionally Intelligent
    - **Self-awareness:** one's own emotions, drives, personality, passions
    - **Self-management:** deferring pleasure, staying power, grit
    - **Social awareness:** other people's emotions and social dynamics
    - **Relationship management:** building and managing positive relationships
2. He Has A Purpose
    - A man who has a purpose is a man who has a WHY[8].
3. He Takes Care Of Himself
    - Eats well
    - Exercises
    - Keeps learning and investing in themselves
4. He Has High Self-Esteem
    - Self-esteem is different from confidence. Your level of confidence fluctuates depending on your results and skills in a given field (I could be confident in my cooking but not

---

[2] Information regarding the traits of a high-quality man provided by power dynamics expert Lucio Buffalmano. See Notes section for more.

in drawing or painting). Self-esteem stays regardless of those external circumstances.
5. He Generates His Own Self-Esteem
   - Some people depend on external forces to boost their ego and self-esteem. High-quality men have more control over their self-esteem.
6. He Has A Secure Attachment Style
   - When a man has a secure attachment style he is emotionally mature. He is also comfortable being vulnerable. Vulnerability ensures that
     a. **He is genuine:** You get to know the real him; he's not wearing any masks
     b. **He is more honest**: he has less need for lies because he has no need to cover his shortcomings
     c. **He is not abusive**: he doesn't need to "prove" his masculinity
7. He Knows Power Dynamics
   - Power moves can be used for good but are commonly used to sneakily sub-communicate who's top dog in the interaction and unfairly assert power over the other person or environment. High-quality men know power dynamics so they can understand the game being played, what's fair and what's not, what's friendly and what's rude, and what they will and will not take. He will then enforce his boundaries accordingly.
8. He Is Honest To His Own Value System
   - High-quality men listen to the advice, feedback, and information of others, but ultimately they build their own value system and have their own moral compass.
9. He Has A Growth Mindset
   - As explained in the introduction, people with a **fixed mindset** believe their qualities are set at birth and carved in stone. You are who you are, and there isn't much you can do about it. People with a **growth mindset** believe they can learn and grow. They *seek* learning and growth opportunities because failing does not define them. On the

contrary, they understand that failing is the only way they can improve.
10. He Takes Responsibility
    - In other words, he has an internal locus of control. The locus of control is the degree to which people believe that they have—or don't have—control over their life. If you have an **internal locus of control**, that means you believe you are in control of your life. Men with an **external locus of control** believe life events determine the course of their life and they don't have control over them.

All of these traits are conducive to a man's ability to acquire resources in life and become (and remain) high-value. These traits also impact your personality, so when you have these traits it shows. Other people see these high-quality traits and perceive you as being high-value. When people perceive you as high-value, they perceive you as high-power. If you're high-warmth when people perceive you as high-power, you'll be "the person everyone wants to be around" and have a much higher success rate in reaching your goals, because everyone will want to have you in their social life. "Everyone" includes powerful people. People will want to network with you, and some of those people will already be high-power themselves.

I hope I'm stating the obvious here, but a higher success rate in networking means you get higher-value connections, which increases *your* value since they are now one of your resources. (To put this another way, your value goes up in the eyes of others when you can name-drop millionaire, billionaire, and celebrity friends.) But it all starts with becoming a high-quality man.

This is what I didn't understand at first. Even when I came to the realization that there were more forms of power than just money, I was missing a large part of the point. The three forms of power in the world are not information, weaponry, and money, but information, weaponry, and resources. "Resources" include money and connections.

To dive a little deeper on this point, there's no telling what you could do with a billionaire for a dad. That's a connection that boosts your value and your power even if you're only connected because you're family. That's still a connection, and you're therefore high-power because of it. If you're not building your connections to grow your power and you are only focusing on money, you're only doing a third of what you could be doing to empower yourself to achieve your goals faster and more effectively. You're using the power of money, but forgetting the power of connections and information.

Most of us don't have billionaires for parents, so boosting our personal power and value through gaining connections starts with boosting the way we are perceived by the people in the world that we want to connect with. Let's go a little deeper on how this works and how you can leverage the fact that perceptions are reality.

"You choose the statement you make to the world with your attitude and appearance. When you choose that statement, you choose how the world will respond to you. If you don't like the way people treat you, you can change that by changing the statement you make to them."**[9]**

What statement are you making to the world right now, with how you carry yourself? If you act like a bully, people will treat you like a bully. If you don't want to be treated like a bully, stop acting like one.

The same logic applies to acting like a high-value man. When first I glanced at the list of traits I would have to develop to be considered a high-quality man, I saw that I had my work cut out for me. It was at this point that I truly had to accept that life is not cured: it's managed. I questioned why I was treated the way I was for so long, hoping the answer would bring me peace. Eventually, I had to accept that regardless of what the answer was, I wasn't going to be able to cure my pain with only one answer, anyway. There is no cure. There is only growth.

To better illustrate this resolution, think of passion. Many people go through life hoping to find their passion by trying different things. Hoping to eventually stumble upon that one thing that makes them happy. Some even hold the belief that once you find something you are truly passionate about, you have found something that you can do everyday without ever encountering feelings of boredom or tiredness.

Know the Power Dynamics

The reality is that your lack of passion and happiness is not "cured" by finding that one thing you've been missing. Passions and happiness are not found; they're developed over time.

In that same respect, I could not be cured—I could only be developed over time. You are the manager of your life, and none of us are born good managers. Good management is an acquired skill. These "high-quality man traits" will help you acquire those skills so you can manage your life in a way that brings you a major step closer to "the good life" (health, wealth, love, and happiness).

This information is not common knowledge, so to avoid confusion understand that high-quality men and high-value men are not exactly the same. While they are similar, the two terms are not interchangeable.

However, while the terms high-quality man and high-value man are not interchangeable, in many ways, a high-quality man is a high-value man. This is because if a high-value man (a man with actual money, connections, and status) does not have any of the traits of a high-quality man, people will have a hard time perceiving him as high-value in the first place.

Imagine a scenario where, at a networking event, you notice a high-value man and a high-quality man speaking with each other. The high-quality man has good posture, his head held high, he smiles warmly, and has a very charming energy about him. He commands respect and elicits positive feelings with his very presence.

As you glance over to the high-value man, you assume he's high-value because he's wearing an expensive watch, but as he speaks to the high-quality man you notice that he can't maintain eye contact. He insecurely glances down with his back hunched and arms crossed defensively. He seems unapproachable, somewhat cold blooded, and seems to be an all-around rude and disrespectful person. (You can't imagine why this high-quality man would want to talk to someone so clearly ill-mannered and impolite.)

The nonverbal expressions (body language) of the high-quality man are ones of leadership and power. He's clearly a dominant man as you notice his more expansive body language. The high-value man, on the other hand, submissively makes himself smaller throughout the conversation.

Now, keep in mind that perceptions are reality. If these two men are complete strangers to you, you may assume that the high-quality man is actually more successful. From the outside looking in, there is no obvious indication that the high-value man contains any traits or qualities needed to acquire resources.

People aren't walking around with their net worth written on their foreheads, so the ones who are perceived as high-power are the ones who carry themselves as if they are. Regardless of what your status or income is, if you dress, walk, talk, and act like a millionaire, people perceive you as one. Conversely, if you dress, walk, talk, and act like a homeless person, people perceive you as one. How you present yourself to people is all they will have to go by as an indicator of your success—unless you share your net worth with everyone you meet.

Now, on the other hand, even if you somehow knew the high-value man was a multimillionaire, his unlikable, unattractive, and displeasing personality gives you the knee-jerk reaction to talk with the high-quality man instead.

Since power is merely the extent to which you can attain what you want, if someone approaches the high-quality man and presents him with an opportunity, he gained an opportunity from a person due to his presentation of his traits as a high-quality man. That means he has a form of power that hard skills can't give you: social power.

This is where "in order to 'have' you must 'do' and in order to 'do' you must be" comes into play. The high-value man skipped the "be" (becoming a high-quality man) and went straight into doing (making money) so he could have (the expensive watch). It's only by deciding to "be" first that you can gain success that lasts and power that doesn't rely on your financial situation or status. In this way, you can achieve social power and create opportunities where others can't.

When people think of power, they only think about high-value men using their money or status to attain what they want, but high-quality men know power dynamics. They know the rules to the game of life. They understand that the world works as a system, and they leverage this system into an advantage that ethically boosts their power over everyone who doesn't know the rules of the game.

As an analogy, we could say that you are the product. You're selling yourself whenever you network and look to build a relationship with someone. The way you present yourself to the world is the marketing. The clothes you wear, the way you talk, walk, move, act, and carry yourself all determine whether or not people will want to buy. High-quality men market themselves as what is arguably the most valuable product in the networking world: high-value (high-power) men.

However, if people are disappointed when they buy a product, they'll return it. In other words, if you lie about being a high-value man through unethical means—such as buying jewelry that is fake gold—when people realize you are not nearly as successful as you claim to be (when people find out who you really are) they'll either stop wanting to connect with you or they will continue conversations with you to be polite but treat you less like an equal and more like a fan. You'll have signaled to them that, in reality, you're low-power. You will have also communicated to them that you are dishonest—which we could say is low-warmth, since it's not a very kind thing to do.

Acquiring the traits of a high-quality man will increase your value and power in real ways, no different from the real effect that removing filler words from your speech pattern has on increasing your verbal influence. (People who avoid using filler words sound more like they know and believe in what they're talking about.)

You'll appear high-power in your social interactions, increasing your ability to attain what you want in life. When you're high-power, you're much harder to ignore. When you're high-power, people feel like they can gain more from a relationship with you and become more willing to join your network.

As you become a high-quality man and better at networking, the principle of authority comes into play. "The principle of authority says we are (much) more likely to listen to someone when we perceive them as having authority." **[10]** When you are a high-quality man who automatically carries himself as a high-value man, people perceive you as having authority. For comparison, in a most extreme situation, a person is more likely to listen to a high-quality man for tips on how to make money than a homeless man with low self-esteem, no purpose, and no personality who doesn't take care of himself.

This was initially a philosophical misunderstanding for me, but it suddenly seemed more like common sense after learning about the power dynamics of my everyday interactions.

Another value I was raised with was to judge people not based on their looks, but based on the content of their character. Maybe that sounds familiar. As a kid, it didn't make sense to me to base worth on looks, age, or success. Wisdom is wisdom. It's not as if the wisdom of saving money is only reserved for people with a net worth of ten million dollars. There are plenty of individuals with an average income who understand how to put away ten percent of their salary each month and can share that knowledge with other people.

Wisdom can also be found in books. It's not like books on personal finance analyze your net worth and then shut automatically with a sign popping out of the cover that says, "You're not worthy of this wisdom." Anyone can receive wisdom, so anyone can share it. So why judge people's wisdom based on how they dress or how they talk? Growing up, I always thought that looks shouldn't matter, because how good you look doesn't affect how much you know.

However, upon learning the principle of authority, it made sense to me why people would ignore the advice of some while acknowledging the advice of others.

I watched an interview with an eight-figure millionaire interviewing a billionaire. The interview was about making money and was intended to give value to its viewers by teaching some rules and basic principles of wealth building. As I scrolled through the comments section of that video, all I saw were comments claiming that the millionaire was talking too much.

I didn't understand how they could be so ungrateful when I could safely assume that little to none of the commenters even had one million and yet, here they were complaining that an eight figure millionaire was talking too much (giving too much advice). The comment that was repeated over and over again was that they wanted to hear more of what the billionaire had to say. The billionaire had a higher net worth, he was higher value, so he had more authority in the field of building wealth. Therefore, they wanted to listen to him more, because people want to listen to the people that they believe have more authority.

As a high-quality man, people perceive you as being high-value. When they perceive you as high-value, you gain a little authority and they are more open to listening to what you have to say. This helps you with your networking, but only if you're willing to leverage the added power that comes with becoming a high-quality man.

In summary, there is power in information and therefore power in this book. In society, the form of power that is most respected and appreciated is resources. You can acquire resources faster by becoming a high-quality man because you'll be perceived as a man with high power and get access to more opportunities from professionals—as long as you mix that high-power with high-warmth. With the acquisition of those resources comes success, which will grow your value and power over time—as long as you follow the rules to the game.

This strategy of becoming a high-quality man for better networking success works for women as well since the main high-quality traits for networking success are emotional intelligence and knowing power dynamics.

Some of you may be led to believe that I am overestimating the power that acquiring the traits of a high-quality man has on the way others perceive and treat you. This is understandable, since the concept of power dynamics is not very well-known and is hardly ever taught in schools. As you progress through this book, you will find further explanations and teachings as to how this process of becoming a high-quality man to achieve your goals works.

If you are already a high-quality man and currently have the power that comes with being high-warmth and high-power, but are still having trouble reaching your goals or getting to that next level, this book is also for you.

Just because everyone wants to be around you, doesn't mean that everyone is willing to do the heavy lifting for you. Not everyone you meet will do all the relationship building for you, nor will they happily create your opportunities with no effort required on your end. The aim of this book is to fill that gap. The aim of this book is to empower you with the best information—the most effective tried-and-true networking strategies—coupled with a plan of action that will give you the ability to go out and get the opportunities you want so you don't wind up waiting around for opportunities to come to you. Follow the program I've laid out in this book and by the end, you'll wonder why you didn't start networking sooner.

Action Steps:

1. On one piece of paper, write down all the traits and subset traits of a high-quality man
   - Ex: Emotional intelligence is a trait. Self-awareness is a subset trait
2. Highlight all the traits and subset traits you currently have
   - Ex: Do you workout daily? If yes, highlight the "Exercise" subset trait underneath the "He Takes Care of Himself" trait
3. On the second piece of paper, create a plan to develop each trait and subset trait you're missing
   - Replace your short-term willpower with a long-term program
   - Ex: When I started out on my journey to becoming a high-quality man, I was lacking social-awareness. A part of my plan to develop that subset trait was to invest in myself with a course that teaches how to read body language and social cues.

Step Two

Adopt the Helpful Mindsets

In the previous chapter, we learned how the people who have the easiest time networking are the people in society that are high in power (high-power). We also learned that, since perceptions are reality, if you present yourself to the world in a way that communicates you are high-power, people will assume that you are. This means that you'll have an easier time networking as well as a higher success rate connecting with powerful contacts.

Before moving further into this chapter, make sure you've placed your self-development and life management as your top priorities. Your mental and physical health must always come first. Take special, attentive care to work on the action steps in the last chapter by improving your daily habits. (For example, one of the traits of a high-quality man is exercising. Exercise can improve your mood.) Look after your mental and emotional health before seeking out networking strategies and opportunities.

Now, we must tackle the conundrum that is mindsets. When I made the decision not to commit suicide, I made a deal with myself: I would do my absolute best to change my life in a way where I could enjoy it again. If, after doing everything I could, I wasn't able to achieve that, I would accept that life just wasn't for everyone.

I tried therapy, and that didn't work out, so I had no idea where to start on my journey to beating my personal demons on my own. Google was giving me advice like "visualize a happy memory"[1], which only made me feel worse when I realized how much things had changed since those happy times.

There were books lying around the house that I always knew were there but had never considered reading. After skimming across a few titles, not even bothering to read the back of the books or open any, I came across a book titled *The Power of Positive Thinking* by Norman Vincent Peale. I decided to give it a chance, and I am so glad I did. The strategies outlined in that book only worked for a little over half a year, but it was enough to engage my curiosity about what else I could learn about mindsets.

As curious as I was, I was still frustrated that I hadn't cured my depression yet. I genuinely thought that with a few positive mindset shifts I would feel better again. That thought was true for the most part, but I hadn't properly anticipated how long making those mindset shifts would take.

When I started practicing things like gratitude, optimism (within proper reason and without the delusion), and healthy positivity, I started to become more productive. Being more positive also helped me network better, since people prefer associating themselves with positive people. This is because positive people are typically higher-warmth than people who are always negative, angry, and intimidating.

A mindset is an established set of attitudes held by a person. However, mindsets can also be seen as arising out of a person's worldview or philosophy of life. For instance, when I had a serious go-giver attitude as a young child, my mindset was to always give, give, give. Always giving was one of my values, one of my life philosophies.

A mindset in this regard is referred to as a frame in social dynamics.

"In social psychology, we can define frames as a set of beliefs, morals, and perspectives with which people interpret the world, or a specific topic."[2]

The concept of frames is also mentioned in Stephen R. Covey's *The 7 Habits of Highly Effective People* but is referred to as a "paradigm."

"The word paradigm comes from the Greek. It was originally a scientific term, and is more commonly used today to mean a model, theory, perception, assumption, or frame of reference. In the more general sense, it's the way we "see" the world—not in terms of our visual sense of sight, but in terms of perceiving, understanding, interpreting."[3]

Adopt the Helpful Mindsets

This is important to understand, because mindsets and frames go hand-in-hand for success at networking. All of our behaviors stem from our mindsets, because it's hard to act outside of our beliefs. For example, if one of your frames is that networking is a complete waste of time and that money is the only way people can get to their goals, your actions will align with that frame and your success rate in networking will go down. Your belief, moral, and perspective with which you interpret the topic of networking isn't conducive to success at networking. If you truly believe networking is a waste of time, it will be hard for you to act outside of that frame (that belief) and suddenly start networking like all your goals depended on it.

It's imperative that you adopt the mindsets and frames that are good for your networking goals. We each have many different frames that we interpret everything through. Those frames can be split into two categories: our frames on how things are ("realities") and our frames of how things should be ("values"). Two frames that you will commonly find on your networking journey are collaborative frames and competitive frames.

When people network within a competitive frame, they are networking with the belief that they have to look out for number one. The lens they use interprets life as a game, a race, a competition. They have to either win it or suffer the consequences that come with losing.[4]

When people network within a collaborative frame, they believe in creating win-win situations. Their frame (the lens they use to view the world) involves benefiting everyone in the relationship and interaction. In other words, they approach networking with the belief that "more for you means more for me, as well."

People who network within a competitive frame don't see things this way. They are influenced by the fixed-pie bias, which is basically the idea that "the more they win, the less there is left for me." Even if their frame of how things should be (values) is that they should be more collaborative, their frame of how things are (realities) leads them to do more taking or else they will "suffer the consequences of losing."

Chris Voss, a former FBI hostage negotiator, says, "Everything in life is a negotiation."[5] The collaborative frame allows you to negotiate for what you want while keeping your eye on ways that you can make the pie bigger for everyone in the process.[6]

Let's take an example that pulls all these ideas together. Let's say you hold a competitive frame while meeting a professional in your industry. Throughout the duration of the entire interaction, your mindset is: what can I gain from this person?

Eventually, he asks you what your goals are. You let him know some of the things that you're working toward and he asks you how he can help support you. He inquires as to how he can help you reach your goal. You both brainstorm ideas, eventually settling on a great deal.

For the sake of this example, let's say that this professional you're talking to is great friends with an expert in graphic design and he's offered to connect you two so you can improve your business cards. You let him know that his offer would be a great help and you thank him for his goodwill, but you don't ask him about his goals. You don't ask how you can help him. You exchange numbers and walk away, feeling good because you gained something; you won. You're operating within a competitive frame, so there's no incentive for you to help anyone but yourself.

Now, it is possible for you to get ahead in life using this competitive frame. The purpose of this book is to give you networking strategies that work, not a lesson on ethics and morality. This strategy could work, and has been proven to work, but only in the short-term. In the long run, you'll be labeled as a "taker" and your behavior will breed distrust. Your actions while networking—even if you're using so-called good human-relations techniques—will be perceived as you only looking out for yourself [7] because your reputation will precede you. Before people see you, they will see your reputation. Having the reputation of someone who is a "taker" will cause people to hesitate to befriend you and eventually diminish your success over the long run.

As we discussed earlier, perceptions are reality. Seeing a woman without a ring on the ring finger of her left hand could lead you to perceive her as unmarried. However, perceiving a married woman as unmarried doesn't change the fact that she's married if she actually is. In that same regard, perceiving competitive frames as superior to collaborative frames doesn't guarantee that competitive frames are superior, especially if they lose their effectiveness over time.

So, what should you do if you have a competitive frame? You could try working on your behavior more—"you could try harder, be more diligent, double your speed. But your efforts would only succeed in getting you to the wrong place faster."[8] This is because you still haven't changed your lens; you're working harder, but using the same unhelpful beliefs and mindsets. To put this a simpler way, you would be networking faster as a taker, and because you still hold a competitive frame, you would only succeed in eroding your chances of long-term success faster. You still believe you have to come out on top, and if you truly believe that, it's illogical for you to start acting collaborative out of nowhere. Our attitudes and behaviors grow out of our assumptions, and your assumption is that you have to be number one. "The way we see things is the source of the way we think and the way we act."[9]

"...conditioning affects our perceptions, our paradigms [frames] ...what about the conditioning of a lifetime? The influences in our lives—family, school, church, work environment, friends, associates, and current social paradigms [social frames]...all have made their silent unconscious impact on us and help shape out frame of reference, our paradigms [frames]..."[10]

We've had our frames conditioned by society our entire lives. We are often unaware that these frames even exist until we choose to deeply examine them. To achieve sustained, lasting success, work within a collaborative frame. Keep an eye on how to make the pie bigger for everyone. Avoid the urge to take as much as you can in an interaction before walking away.

While collaboration is what I strongly recommend (since collaborative frames are superior to competitive frames in the long run), your "why" is the determining factor of which frame you decide would work best for you.

THE CLEVER CONNECTOR

Your "why," your reason for working hard to get better at networking, your reason for working hard to build a strong network, and your reason for wanting to achieve your goals, is important for your productivity. It is also important for your ultimate decision on what approach you want to take to networking. Your why has four different levels. **[11]**[3]:

1. Survival
   - "The first level of why is survival. Let me explain what I mean by survival: Everybody who has a job that makes money is making that money why? To survive and pay bills. When people make enough money to pay their bills and cover their mandatory living expenses, some people stop there and never graduate."
2. Status
   - "The second level of why is all about status. You'll hear people say things like, 'You know, I want to make six figures.' Why? Status. Or they may want a nice car, house, or to go to a good school. They want to be able to talk about having this or that. This is all about keeping up with the Joneses. Status is still lightweight, but it's better than survival."
3. Freedom
   - "The third level of why is freedom. People may say, 'You know what? I'm so sick and tired of six figures. Man, I want to be free. I want to make money. I'm not worried about working hard, I want to make money and I want to have freedom. I want to have some breathing room. What do I need to do to have breathing room?' They may want to live in a particular community because they want their kids to be able to play outside and not have to worry about them. Or they may want to have a big backyard so their kids can run around and play safely."

---

[3] Information regarding the four whys provided by author and entrepreneur Patrick Bet-David. See Notes section for more.

4. Purpose
    - "The highest level is purpose. Now what are we talking about with purpose? Some people say, 'My why is to one day own a football team.' That's still empty. Is that really the purpose of making millions or billions of dollars? No. There's got to be a bigger purpose. So how does one go from survival, status, freedom, to purpose? What is truly your purpose? What's your purpose? What is the bigger picture? When your why is purpose, you know what you're driven by. But that doesn't happen overnight. As the saying goes, sometimes on the way to a dream, you get lost and find a bigger one. A bigger dream. It takes time, patience, self-discovery, and experience. You think it was all about the car. You think it was all about the recognition. You think it was all about the fame. You think it was all about the status. You think it was all about landing that girl. You think it's all about all these other things, but it's much bigger than that. Then all of a sudden, one day you have a conversation with somebody or watch a video or a movie, or you meet someone and boom; it just hits you in the face, and you realize what you were put on this planet to do. Now you're talking purpose."

To illustrate my point, if your "why" is survival and you only care to do well enough in life to get by, maybe you don't care about the long term. In that case, you might read this book and walk away with the decision to hold a competitive frame and maybe that frame will help you achieve that goal. After all, the takers of this world make money, too. But for anyone who has a why any level above survival, networking within a collaborative frame is the most effective and beneficial mindset for the achievement of your goals.

When you know your why, and you've decided on your frame of choice, you can start networking with more intention and clarity on your approach. But even though your networking is intentional (because you know your why) and strategic (because you have clarity on what frame you're networking with), that doesn't mean you'll be networking confidently.

Being a confident networker is important. We already established how important it is to be perceived as high-power. A strong indicator of who is the most powerful in an interaction or a group is whoever the leader is. Powerful people lead. It's uncommon to see weak people with low self-esteem who are also effective and influential leaders. Your typical powerful leader is usually confident in themselves and has a healthy ego. That means if you want to be perceived as powerful, you need to be (or at the very least, appear to be) confident while you're networking.

In society, people tend to make the mistake of conflating confidence and self-esteem. The two are often (incorrectly) used interchangeably. Confidence is your trust in a single ability. In other words, where I could be confident in my ability to cook, I may not be confident in my skydiving abilities, because I've never skydived before. Self-esteem is defined by how highly you value yourself. If you don't respect or love yourself very much, you would be defined as having low self-esteem. What you need to understand is that because most people see confidence and self-esteem as the same thing, by developing your self-esteem, you will be perceived as more of a high-quality man and as a confident networker.

Being a confident networker doesn't just help you appear more powerful; it also helps you appear as though you have been networking for a long time. Since confidence is your trust in a single ability, if you are confident while networking, people will see that you trust your ability to network and begin to see you as having more authority in the art and field of networking. This is definitely an added benefit, because authority helps build your networking success.

Once again, "The principle of authority states that we are (much) more likely to listen to someone when we perceive them as having authority. Especially if we're dealing in his field of supposed expertise[12]." When you introduce yourself with confidence, build relationships with confidence, and use effective networking strategies that show you know what you're doing, people perceive you as having authority in networking. This gives the impression that you've networked many times before and leads them to believe that you are high-power. After all, if you meet someone who always knows the right thing to say and networks like they've done it a thousand times before, chances are you would wonder how big their network is and what kind of connections they have.

This is the effect you have on others when you're networking with high self-esteem and sound networking strategies. They take you more seriously. They may even wonder what kinds of powerful connections you might have to be so confident while building professional relationships with people you have never met before. But it all starts with having the high self-esteem of a high-quality man.

To gain this power, you must develop the traits "He Generates His Own Self-Esteem" and "He Has a Growth Mindset" that high-quality men have. You must cultivate an antifragile ego.[4]

"Antifragile, as defined by Nassim Taleb, doesn't mean strong and it's not even a synonym of strong. 'Strong' is defined by its breaking point, while antifragile means that the more you attack it, the stronger it gets[13]." To generate a self-esteem that doesn't rely on external forces and circumstances that are always in your favor, you must build an identity that is antifragile and derive your self-esteem from that identity[14].

"Most of us form our self-esteem around two typical identities and one event. The first identity is being good at something (meaning: their ego/identity is 'I'm good at X'); the second is 'being good in general' (meaning: 'I'm a great fella'). The event is usually achieving a certain goal (meaning: getting that job, making X money, sleeping with that person etc.). Being good at X becomes a bit like adopting a fixed mindset. You start becoming defensive about your defining qualities, because failing at them would mean showing, to you and to others, that you are not good after all. That means that you get worried about failing. That means you stop experimenting, and trying and learning and growing. That means you slowly start building your own mental straight jacket. Not good. And what if something happens and you're not good anymore? Or if you have to switch fields, or a bunch

---

[4] Data and information regarding the anti-fragile ego provided by essayist and author Nassim Nicholas Taleb and power dynamics expert Lucio Buffalmano. See Notes section for more.

of new and more skilled people enter the scene? Identity crisis! The solution?"**[15]**

"When you build your ego around antifragile qualities you shield yourself from plateauing and from ever becoming defensive of the status quo. Here are some examples of antifragile identities:

- I'm an eternal learner
- I go for it and do my best no matter the situation
- Winning is great, but the real art, poetry, and beauty is in the struggle
- My worst moments are my best learning experiences (and fuel to achieve more)
- I love reality, even when it's not good. Especially when it's not good
- I'm a gritty mofo and I never stop

See what the beauty of these is? The more difficulties you throw at them, the more chances you have to validate yourself. Your pride grows when you move forward. These identities you pick for yourself are aligned with eternal self-development (and greatly increase the likelihood of your success)."**[16]**

You have to be willing to fail to learn. You have to be willing to learn to grow. You grow in order to become the kind of person capable of achieving their goals, but it all starts with being willing to fail. Now, that doesn't mean that your antifragile ego will make failing totally painless; failing still hurts. But now you'll have the self-esteem to get up and go again.

The antifragile ego is connected to networking in more ways than just how people perceive you. The antifragile ego helps you understand and internalize that networking is an art form. It takes practice, just like any other art form. There will be moments in networking where you don't succeed in building that relationship or connection you wanted, but now you can detach your identity from always needing to win. You will have more personal and mental power than those who must win to protect their ego and feel good about themselves.

Adopt the Helpful Mindsets

Achieving "the good life"—achieving health, wealth, love, and happiness—requires self-development. Self-development demands you grow as a person. Growth requires learning lessons, and learning lessons requires failure.

Whenever I'm afraid to send an email to a top-dog in my niche or cold-call a celebrity, I think to myself, "I take pride not in doing things perfectly, but in having the courage to do it even when it's far from perfect."**[17]** Then, I send that email and I make that call. As a result, many of the people whom I connected with were surprised I had the confidence to reach out to them without the help of a mutual friend introducing me. Little did they know, it wasn't confidence. It was high self-esteem and a healthy ego.

I used the antifragile ego to work on my progress toward becoming a high-quality man. Throughout my personal journey to becoming a high-quality man, when I worked on the action steps in the last chapter, I realized that I needed to work on my personality. I wanted a personality that was masculine, because I wanted to be and feel like a "real man." Not having a father figure as a good role model for most of my life, I did my own research on what it took to become a man. I began by searching for a deeper understanding of masculinity through my exploration of male psychology.[5]

"The age-old concepts of masculinity involve being abusive or domineering. But mature masculinity is instead generative, creative, and empowering of the self and others. The four mature male archetypes that stand out through myth and literature across history are: the king (the energy of just and creative ordering), the warrior (the energy of aggressive but nonviolent action), the magician (the energy of initiation and transformation), and the lover (the energy that connects one to others and the world)."**[18]**

"The King is the 'executive', mature masculine personality. It makes the decisions and is grounded in his own reality – he serves as a rock in times of trouble. Men that have fully developed The King

---

[5] Information regarding male psychology provided by authors Douglas Gillette and Robert L. Moore and author Jon Anthony. See Notes section for more.

archetype of masculinity live with integrity, protect their kingdom (friends, family, etc.), and bless others. He also embodies creative energy, with a joy so strong that he wants to share it with others."[19]

"The Lover is not merely concerned with sex, however—The Lover, in its fullness, has a deep love for life itself. Love for family, for friends, for food, for reading, for activity and for progression; the Lover is passionate in whatever he does. The Lover is sensual, and enjoys all types of (healthy) pleasure; good food and drink, beautiful art, poetry, songs, sex, and others."[20]

"The Magician is the masculine personality that deals with knowledge and wisdom. The Magician personality manifests itself when you try to solve a problem, introspect, or improve your life with knowledge. The Magician is the master of technology and of mastery; he enjoys gaining new skills and knowledge not only so that he can better his life, but also because he simply enjoys expanding his mind."[21]

"The Warrior personality is that assertive, aggressive, masculine energy that wants to conquer things and further its cause. The Warrior manifests itself when you hustle and struggle to improve yourself; he is the personality of purpose. (Without the Warrior archetype in its fullness, you cannot embody your masculine purpose.)"[22]

At the time, I was working on developing the Warrior archetype of masculinity. I started taking cold showers to improve my mental discipline and strength of will (struggling to improve myself). The problem was, I would turn on the water and then second guess stepping inside to put myself through that immense physical torment. To gain the strength I needed, I would shut my brain off, jump in, and as the cold water cascaded over my body I would say to myself, "I am proud of myself every time I show up to a difficult situation because I am able to prove and validate to myself my strength of character while growing my personal power."[23]

With that antifragile identity in mind, I was able to resist the immense urge to reach for the temperature knob and develop a consistent cold shower habit, finishing my cold showers strong and emotionally rewarding myself after stepping out to a bathroom that was warmer outside the shower than inside.

Now that we've established the topics of frames and the self-esteem of a high-quality man more in-depth, we can transition into another important part of your mindset: motivation.

Having the ability to stay motivated to complete and achieve your goals with your "why" in mind is important for your productivity, success, and inner feelings of fulfillment. To do that, find what motivates you and use it to your advantage to bring out the best in yourself. Here is a list of the twenty things that motivate people, separated into four categories:**[24]**[6]

4 Areas That Drive People

Advancement – These people see reaching new heights as the best form of motivation.

1. Next Promotion

If all you want to do is hit your next promotion, sit down with a team leader or teammate and figure out what goals you need to accomplish to get there.

2. Completing a Task

"These are the people that have to finish what they've started." If you are like that, break down your responsibilities into tasks so you can stay motivated.

3. Meeting a Deadline

"Some people are only motivated by a looming deadline. A deadline gives them a clear goal to focus on and many of them work up until the last second before the deadline is reached." If this is you, give yourself more deadlines or move the deadline sooner to get more results.

---

[6] Data and information regarding the 20 things that motivate people provided by author and entrepreneur Patrick Bet-David. See Notes section for more.

4. Reaching a Goal as a Team

"Not everyone on the team is going to be the MVP, many people are motivated by the team reaching new heights together." If, as a leader, you're on a team and are motivated by reaching a goal as a team, you have to give your team increasing milestones to keep yourself and these types of people motivated because they thrive on team success.

Individual – These people see personal goals and wants as the best form of motivation.

5. Lifestyle

"This person likes nice things, but they aren't selfish in a negative sense. People that are driven by achieving a lifestyle know what they want to get out of working hard. Their goal is tangible. Motivating yourself if you're driven by a certain lifestyle is about understanding what your end goal looks like."

6. Recognition

Let's say you're an employer working with employees that are driven by recognition. "Motivating them becomes all about making the extra effort to turn the spotlight on them whenever you can. They will shine and outperform everybody if they are given recognition for their performance. It could be as simple as having a one-on-one and letting them know how much you appreciate the effort they are putting out there."

7. Security

"There are people out there that selfishly want to be secure in their job, their lifestyle, or in their industry. These people want to live in communities and countries that provide them with a sense of security. If this is you, you're motivated by security."

Madness – These people see unconventional factors as the best form of motivation.

8. Opposition

"These top performers need someone to go up against, they need opposition." In certain environments, if this is you, presenting yourself with what your opposition can do will motivate you to perform at a high level. (Find out what your opposition is capable of to be motivated by the challenge of going up against them.)

9. Competition

"Create a competitive environment for yourself and see if you live off the competition. Pit yourself against the competitive people to bring out the best performance you have. This is not about being combative, this is about competing as motivation to win."

10. Control

"If you're an employer managing employees, you may notice that some employees want to control their space, their team, or their industry. Gaining and keeping control over their area is what drives them to win. You can tell these people what they can do to put themselves in control of what they are doing."

11. Power and Fame

"There were a lot of people that said, 'I want to go make my money because after making my money, I want to go run for governor,' or 'I want to be able to have the power and the influence to be on the cover of Time magazine and make some big decisions.' Some people might think that fame isn't the noblest thing to pursue, but this is about getting the best out of yourself. If this is what you're motivated by, you need to learn the right values and the right principles that will allow you to apply all of these motivations positively."

12. Proving Others Wrong

"Barbara Corcoran is a great example of this type of person. Her ex-boyfriend told her that she wouldn't achieve anything without him. So, she left him, built and sold a million-dollar company, and is now on Shark Tank every week. If this is you, proving others wrong lights a fire under you to motivate you to win."

13. The Need to Avoid Embarrassment

"If this is you, you're the kind of person who over prepares for a speech because you need to nail this speech so badly to avoid embarrassing yourself. You are going to go above and beyond, to avoid the situation, because your need is so great."

14. Mastery

"Mastery is a little different from control. Mastery is about being the best in all aspects. There isn't a technique, history lesson, or new technology these people don't know about. It requires repetition and a lot of time. If masters publicly told you their schedules, you would be frightened of them. 99.9% of people don't want to be a master because of the commitment. Masters are crazy."

15. Be the Best [Break Records]

"It isn't mastery or control. These people are motivated by shattering records that other people have achieved. They want their name at the top of every category, or to walk into a room with their peers and have everyone stand in awe of them. It doesn't matter how they do it, they only care about achieving it. They want to be the very best like no one ever was."

Purpose – These people see something bigger than themselves as the best form of motivation.

16. History

"People that are driven by history want to be remembered long after they are dead. They don't want to be like the countless long-dead billionaires that nobody remembers. They think it's great that those dead billionaires achieved wealth, but to people driven by history, it's legacy that matters to them."

17. Helping others

"The motivation to serve others is about taking the wealth and success you gain and using it to benefit the community. Whether it is giving time and money back to those less fortunate or mentoring young entrepreneurs on their way up, serving others motivates people to perform."

18. Change

"If you're a team leader, you may notice change is a driving factor for some of your teammates. They want to change an industry, a process, the way we view the world or even change what goals the team may have. Change as a motivator comes down to results and how you, as a team leader, help these change agents reach the results they are excited about."

19. Impact

"For some people, they don't want to come in and fill a role or a seat. They want to make an impact that is lasting for the company or team. It is about creating a ripple effect that spreads far and wide."

20. Enlightenment

"Enlightened people ask, 'How can I get myself to be more enlightened by gathering information and data, so I can help make better decisions?' Once you provide them with the right knowledge, everything clicks, and they drive growth."

Find which of these motivations resonate with you, then double down on them. Try to make them tangible. For example, if you're motivated by helping others, you can fill out a check for $1,000,000 and make it out to (pay to the order of) your favorite charity. Then put it on your wall where you can see it every day.

If you're motivated by recognition, you can hire someone to photoshop you on a Time magazine and print that magazine to keep somewhere you'll see it every day. Get creative. I know people who were motivated by lifestyle and bought Lamborghini keys to put at their work desk to motivate them to be more productive. Find what works for you, then leverage that.

When I was getting started, I used "dark motivation." These are thoughts filled with anger about how I would get enough success to get back at anyone who ever mistreated me.

This is a warning: be very careful with dark motivation! It can increase your productivity but hurt the quality of your results if taken too far. Usually dark motivation causes you to be productive for the wrong reasons. It can develop into a toxic mindset if the dark motivation is held onto for too long and you never provide yourself with the closure you need to move forward with a more healthy motivation as fuel (accepting that your partner cheated on you, accepting that your father was never there, etc.).

For me, "dark motivation" came from a time when I had just become an actor and won my first acting award. My mother told me, "The entertainment industry isn't going to want some skinny black kid with kidney failure, and nobody's going to want to hire some black kid with a GED. I hope you enjoy getting raped in jail." My mother had no problem expressing what she thought about me on a daily basis in different abusive ways.

You can imagine how I must have felt hearing those things. I had already decided not to commit suicide, but she wasn't making that decision easy. There were days when she told me I "have the devil inside of me", days when she went through my wallet and stole from me, and eventually there came a day when she kicked me out of the house and I was forced to find somewhere else to stay or be homeless.

I took all of my pain and turned it into motivation, but this became toxic to my mental health. Success became all that mattered and it ended up holding me back, because that mindset made me less of a high-quality man and less strategic in my decision making. My emotions clouded my judgement because of my mindsets that were rooted in dark motivation. I was working all the time and hardly talking to anyone. This caused my personality to suffer again which, as you know, is one of the subset traits of emotional intelligence, an important component to being a high-quality man.

I gradually learned to let go of that pain and transition into healthier forms of motivation. That is only one of the many ways dark motivation can screw your chances of achieving your goals. Avoid making the same mistake I did by letting dark motivation fester and build up uncontrollably.

Here is another alternative to dark motivation so you can have a better time staying on the right mental track. In the book *The Adversity Advantage* by Paul G. Stoltz, Ph.D., and Erik Wihenmayer, Stoltz makes the point that, "You cannot elevate anyone or anything to its highest potential without adversity." Stoltz then references the term "AQ" which stands for "Adversity Quotient." Stoltz says, "Your Adversity Quotient (AQ) is a measure of how you respond to adversity of all kinds, or how you react to the world around you."**[25]**.

To develop a higher adversity quotient and become better at not just handling adversity but turning adversity into fuel (healthy motivation), here are a couple of techniques you can use:**[26]**[7]

"The Summit Game – Envision yourself at the finish line."

You're motivated by that "Next Promotion." Let's say you've decided to create a tangible motivator, as I recommended earlier, by keeping a letter on your work desk that you typed up and printed out. That letter is from the company you work for, offering you a promotion. When you face adversity and that tangible motivator isn't enough, you can envision yourself in that new position you're working toward, performing the activities unique to that position—such as leading a team or giving a presentation. You can envision the raise you'll receive in addition to that promotion and imagine receiving your first check, a large step up in pay from what you were making.

---

[7] Information regarding the Adversity Quotient concept and ways to raise one's Adversity Quotient provided by authors Paul G. Stoltz, Ph.D., and Erik Wihenmayer. See Notes section for more.

"The Failure Fantasy – Fuel from the thought of failure."

This is the exact opposite of the Summit Game. If, for example, you're motivated by the need to avoid embarrassment, envision yourself failing miserably and being harassed severely for it. Imagine being kicked out of the social circle of everyone who saw your embarrassing failure and imagine feeling isolated, with no one to talk to, no support, no friends or family. Imagine becoming all alone because you didn't do what it took to succeed.

To build on this topic of your why and your motivations, you may be wondering why you lack the will or motivation to work toward your goals with your "why" in the first place. This question is reminiscent of the same questions posed by members of our older generation who find it hard to manage millennials. They ask, "Why don't millennials want to work hard?" Older college deans who notice students who seem underdeveloped and ill-prepared for the journey ahead ask, "Why don't students want to grow up?"

Tim Elmore provides the following theory as a response: "the adult world you are entering has never been more complex, and the older generation is not adequately preparing you for what you will soon face. Furthermore, the adolescent world has never been more pleasurable. Many in the Generation Y demographic see no need to leave their current reality of leisure to enter a long, hard adult lifestyle."[27]

To overcome these issues set by circumstances you can't control, here are some tips to keep you headed on the right track with a solid work ethic:

Be Prepared to Work Hard. Be Prepared for Adversity.

No surprises. Avoid letting the size of your workloads catch you off guard. Figure out a good number on a scale of one to ten that accurately estimates how much work you'll have to put in. Then, double that number.

On my journey, there were times when I was encouraged to take the easy route and give up on my dreams. One example is the night my mother stole money from me. I pretended to be asleep as I heard my door creak open. Out of the corner of my eye, I saw her approach my night stand, open my wallet, and leave abruptly, closing my door softer than how she opened it. I would get up, shine my phone light into my wallet, and find that money was missing. The same money I needed to move closer to my goals was now gone. Fighting with my mother would result in me getting kicked out, so I had no choice but to start over and work harder. My only other option was giving up, and I had made up my mind not to let that happen.

When my kidney failure struck, I was in my sophomore year at a private high school. I missed so much school due to my long hospitalization that I had to do summer school if I wanted to keep my sophomore year credits. This private high school was in a different county, so I would wake up at four in the morning to get ready for school, make the two-hour drive with my dad, work throughout the day, then do homework on the two hour drive back so I could get enough sleep by the time I got home to wake up early again. Needless to say, transferring to a public school that was closer to home was a smarter choice given my newfound health situation.

When I transferred schools, the private high school decided that they would not release my high school transcripts with my two years worth of high school credits unless I paid a $1,000 transfer fee. Money that I did not have.

The funny thing is, I didn't receive this important information until I was in my senior year of high school. So, take a guess what happened. I'm in my senior year of high school working to acquire three years worth of credits. The only credits I had that remained were from my junior year. Keep in mind that this public school wasn't the best. Some of the teachers were racist toward me and grouped me in with the majority of African-American students doing drugs, selling drugs, stealing school equipment from the music room to launch their rap careers, and getting sent to jail for one reason or another.

What do you think I did? Do you think I dropped out? I worked hard. Online classes became my best friend. No one thought I would graduate. A few months after my mother found out my situation, it was then, as we stood in the kitchen, that she stopped and said, "No one is going to want to hire some black kid with a GED. I hope you enjoy getting raped in jail."

THE CLEVER CONNECTOR

What do you think I did? I got angry, naturally, but I didn't give up. I worked harder. Eventually, I graduated with my high school diploma. But it all started with my being prepared to work hard.

When I first decided to become an actor, I was working as a cashier at a grocery store. I had enrolled in a modeling and acting class that cost me $2,145 in tuition. Luckily, I could split the payment into six monthly payments of $350.

I was the only African-American in the grocery store and also the only person making $9.25 per hour. Everyone else was making $10 per hour or above. I asked my boss for a raise, doing my best to reason with her that I had been working for over a year and deserved it. She denied my request.

I worked eight-hour shifts, picking up extra shifts from anyone who "called out". Having kidney failure with no transplant or dialysis made that daily work rough on my body. Toxins compounded inside of me that my kidneys weren't strong enough to clear out, making me sick, sluggish, physically weak, and tired. I woke up early, worked eight hours, went home, and practiced my acting until midnight. Then, I would repeat.

Once, my boss didn't give me enough hours to pay off the acting class's full monthly payment. If I couldn't make that payment, I would get kicked out of the school. I asked my mother for help, but she didn't support my goal. She told me if I couldn't make the payment I should drop out. This is when, in her living room, she told me, "The entertainment industry wouldn't want to hire some skinny black kid with kidney failure." My father didn't believe in me at the time either, but was willing to loan me $100.

Eventually, through consistent hard work, I did it. I made all the payments and completed all the classes. In the final class, all the students were invited to join an acting competition. The only problem was, the competition had a $1,000 registration fee. I had already poured all the money I had into the classes, and I barely made the $350 payments. The registration fee deadline was so close. Luckily, I was prepared to work hard.

I grinded every day. There was still no kidney transplant yet and no dialysis to remove the toxins from my body that were slowing me down. I had to rely on my strength of will and my work ethic to keep me going. I would take customers to my register as a worn-out cashier, then practice my acting at that same register when things slowed down later in the day (when I had fewer customers to assist). People thought I was mentally unstable because I was talking to myself, but they didn't know I was training for the big day. They didn't know my dreams, they didn't know my goals, and they certainly didn't know the sacrifices I was being forced to make, so it didn't make a whole lot of sense to me to care about what they thought.

My mother called my boss and told her to cut my hours. When I found out, my mother told me that I should be spending less time at work and more time cleaning her house. My parents were going through a divorce that hadn't been officialized yet, and she was taking her pain out on me. Her explanation for not giving back my hours after I cleaned her house was that I "had the devil inside me." With the odds of me making the money I needed being so slim, I could have given up right then and there. But I was prepared to work hard.

After my long work days, I would walk home, eat dinner, and work on writing the commercial I would perform at the competition. I would act in the mirror, revise the script, rewrite the script, and work until midnight only to wake up early the next day and go back to work.

My mother didn't want to drive me to the competition, so I went with my dad. There were roughly three hundred contestants and about forty judges.

I won the entire competition, with over twenty-one callbacks from the judges and an acting scholarship as icing on the cake. I was proud. My hard work had paid off. My dad had tears in his eyes as he told me that after everything I had been through, I deserved that win. That was the first time I had ever seen my dad cry. He called my mother and told her the news, and she drove the same two hours she didn't want to drive to take me to the competition location to brag to the other parents that I was her son.

Two weeks later, she made another phone call and cancelled the scholarship. I begged her to give it back but she smiled and told me that I wasn't going to go and ride off into the sunset with my father.

She was assuming my father and I were going to be successful off of my acting career. My father told her to leave me out of their divorce situation but she didn't listen. I told her I would do anything if she would give me the scholarship back, but she said she didn't want anything from me. I searched for my passport and birth certificate to see if I could call the department and verify my identity to get it back somehow. Turns out she took my passport and birth certificate, as well as my father's, and hid them. I ended up losing the scholarship.

I was still prepared to work hard. I emailed every judge that gave me a callback and did online research to get the contact info of all the other judges who attended. Regardless of if they gave me a callback, regardless of if they were interested in me or not, I sent them an email and got on their radar.

Eventually, I got an email back from a producer who aired the whole competition on TV. Since I won, that producer was open to interviewing me on her show and with the help of my dad, we made it happen. I had my first credit on my acting resume and an opportunity that opened the doors to many others, but it all started with being prepared to work hard.

You may think that was a lot of work for my ill body to endure, but then you'd only be seeing half the story.

The work I put in to achieve the accomplishments I have today took more than just physical strength: it took mental strength, as well. That means that whatever idea you have in your head of how much work you're expecting to have to put in, take that idea and double it. Now you won't be surprised when the work comes, and you won't be shocked out of working harder when that hard work becomes hell.

Leverage the Psychological Benefit of Mottos

"Mottos can replace destructive thinking with healthy self-talk, help you change a habit, remind you of who you are and what you stand for, jog your conscience, remind you of your values, teach character strengths, provide a bracing shot of inspiration, calm your mind, increase your productivity, and keep you focused on your long-term

Adopt the Helpful Mindsets

goal."[28] Here are some good military mottos to help you on your mission:[29][8]

1. Stay Alert, Stay Alive
   - I used this when I was working on changing my habits. I kept track of what time of day I would usually be overcome by a sugar craving and set an alarm for fifteen minutes before that time. When that alarm went off, it showed the motto "Stay Alert, Stay Alive" to remind me the craving was coming. By predicting it, it couldn't catch me off guard and I could choose to eat healthier food or do something else productive instead.
2. Whatever it Takes
   - You would think that the one thing that kills dreams in driven individuals is fear and self-doubt, but the real dream killer is boredom. Driven individuals are driven towards their goals and want to experience those big achievements. As a result, they typically don't care for the mundane, everyday tasks that must be completed to get there. The unattractive and unexciting cleaning-out of your email inbox that you had determined to do to stay more organized suddenly became a more daunting task than you had originally bargained for. In moments like this, I had to tell myself, "Whatever It Takes."
3. The Only Easy Day Was Yesterday
   - As I previously said earlier, be prepared to work hard. Expect mental and emotional pain, tiredness, and grueling hard work today, because "The Only Easy Day Was Yesterday."
4. Molon Labe (Come and Take Them)
   - "Come and take them." Come and take away my dreams, my ability to achieve my goals, my ability to prove my enemies wrong, my ability to gain recognition, my ability to

---

[8] Information regarding military mottos provided by author and entrepreneur Patrick Bet-David. See Notes section for more.

help others, my ability to make history. "Come and take them." I dare you.

5. Better to Die, Than to Be a Coward
    - This is similar to the antifragile ego. You can use this motto in addition to adopting the identity of a learner. When you're afraid to approach that CEO, remember that it's "Better to Die, Than to Be a Coward."
6. Facta non Verba (Deeds, Not Words)
    - Actions speak louder than words. If you want to achieve that goal, say less and do it. Everybody says, "This year is going to be my year." Everybody says, "It's my time now." Say less. "Deeds, Not Words."
7. Si vis pacem, para bellum (If You Wish for Peace, Prepare for War)
    - Become a high-quality man so you can avoid the problems that arise when people perceive you as not being worth their time. When you are and act like a high-quality man, people perceive you as high-value. They want to network with you because they have no idea how high your net worth might be, or who you might know. What you don't want is to be the guy who approaches professionals and is treated like a fan instead of being respected as an equal. If you wish for that respect, that peace, "Prepare for War" by becoming a high-quality man first so it doesn't have to come to that.
8. Lerne leiden ohne zu klagen (Learn to Suffer Without Complaining)
    - Hard work is exactly that: hard work. You're going to fail on your journey to success, and you're going to suffer. My favorite place to use this military motto is in the gym. When I'm in the middle of a set and my body feels like it can't go on, when my mind is telling me that I've done enough, I remember this motto: "Learn to Suffer Without Complaining." After all, I'm a learner, and that's a damn good thing to learn.
9. No Mission Too Difficult, No Sacrifice Too Great. Duty First

Adopt the Helpful Mindsets

- I usually use this motto when I'm deep in thought about my goals. My why is at the "Purpose" level, so I set the bar high for myself and, as a result, have ambitious goals. When I would think about the size of those goals and how far away those goals were in comparison to where I was, it was easy for me to feel like I was definitely going to stay on this path toward achieving my goals. However, I wasn't sure if I would be able to actually achieve it in the end. It was easy, at times, for me to want to sit down and watch TV instead of getting work done. It was easy for me to make the excuse to myself that I could use the break. At times like those, when I need to remember that sacrifice is the difference between success and failure, then I say the motto to myself: "No Mission Too Difficult, No Sacrifice Too Great. Duty First." I can and will achieve it in the end, and before taking that undeserved break, it's duty first. The mission comes first. My why must come first.

10. The Hard We Shall Do Today, the Impossible We Shall Do Tomorrow
    - I like to use this one in moments when I'm already feeling motivated or inspired. When you take the hard route day in and day out, making the hard choices every day, eventually you'll do something that everyone will say was impossible. In reality, the "impossible" was nothing more than the compound effect of you continuously making the hard choice, doing the hard things, every day. So, when I'm feeling motivated, I say, "The Hard We Shall Do Today, the Impossible We Shall Do Tomorrow," and go make the hard choice with a smile on my face.

One of the ways this chapter will help you move forward in terms of your networking capability is in your overall networking performance. In Daniel Pink's 2009 book *Drive* he describes the Keys to Performance as Autonomy, Mastery, and Purpose.[30]

"Autonomy is the need to direct your own life and work. To be fully motivated, you must be able to control what you do, when you do it, and who you do it with."[31] You have autonomy in terms of being able to decide whether or not you want to network, when you want to network, and who you want to network with. By becoming a high-quality man, you'll also be able to further understand the power of autonomy and get it.

"Mastery is the desire to improve. If you are motivated by mastery, you'll likely see your potential as being unlimited, and you'll constantly seek to improve your skills through learning and practice."**[30]** If you've stuck with me through the book this far and have started working on becoming a high-quality man by taking the action steps outlined at the end of the previous chapter, then chances are you have a desire to improve and are somewhat motivated by mastery. You may have also adopted the antifragile ego and built your identity around being a learner.

Purpose is when "people may become disengaged and demotivated at work if they don't understand, or can't invest in, the 'bigger picture.'"**[31]** Since you discovered your why already as well as your motivations, you have the bigger picture in mind already. This picture can serve as a roadmap to tell you where you want to go and what roads will (and won't) take you there.

While this is all good and means you will perform at a much higher level, mindset shifts and changes in how you view the world are not instantaneous. They often take time and can be a grueling process.

Many people make the mistake of trying to work on only their outward behaviors without touching their mindset. In other words, if someone held the frame that networking is a total waste of time and energy and provides no ability to advance your career, they might try to network anyway without changing their belief (their frame). However, "both your attitude and your behavior while networking are going to be congruent with the way you see networking because our frames, our beliefs, are the source of our attitudes and behaviors, so it's hard to act with integrity outside of them."**[32]**

This is why one thing to keep in mind as you network is the importance of networking. Just because you know why you want to achieve your goals doesn't mean you fully understand why networking is a good vehicle to get you there.

Adopt the Helpful Mindsets

I had to become more aware of my frames and assumptions and become aware of the extent to which I had been influenced by my experiences so I could take responsibility for those frames, examine them, and test them against reality. That meant I had to change my frame to one that took networking more seriously as a method for getting to the top.

The highest achievers know and understand that a good network means proven and specialized knowledge whenever you need it. People come across problems they don't know how to solve every day and stress themselves out over figuring out the best course of action to take. Having a good network means you don't need to have the answers, you only need to know someone else who does.

High achievers also know that networking means more opportunities, influence, and income. When you network properly, people want to work with you. The bigger your network, the more opportunities, which means more income and more success. With bigger players in your network, you expand your influence because you become higher power. This leads to you being able to create opportunities if you aren't satisfied with the amount you're getting from your network, because people will begin to see you the same way you see celebrities. There are even situations where you are rewarded for introducing or connecting two people to help them solve each other's problems. In those situations, a good networker is rewarded twice, once by each party, since you helped them both by connecting them to each other and they were both able to benefit from the introduction.

A good network also means time saved. The young people who focus on making more money to achieve their goals typically take longer to achieve them. The young people who focus on building their network in addition to making money cut their learning curve in half, saving time by learning from professionals who have proven that they know what they're talking about.

As I changed my frames and saw networking differently, I began to think differently and feel differently about networking as a vehicle to success. I also began to think differently about my ability to reach my goals faster with the right people in my corner. This caused me to behave differently. I didn't have to worry about controlling my outward attitude or behaviors because my entire mindset had changed. It all started with controlling and changing my frames. I didn't have to worry about controlling my attitude or my behavior; I was filled with wonder and motivation, determined to discover just how far I could go if I included millionaires, billionaires, and celebrities into my network.

As I developed a more well-rounded respect for networking, I had to wonder: what would have happened if I had had a high-quality man in my network when I had my near-death experience? Maybe he could have taught me that the way my friends treated me at that time was nothing personal. How much pain and suffering could I have avoided? How much time could I have put into becoming a high-quality man myself instead of asking so many "why" questions that I never got the answer to? All those suicidal thoughts could have been a lot easier to overcome if I had known the world played by rules I hadn't followed. I had to find out the hard way years after dealing with my emotional trauma.

My mother told me to never tell anyone about the things that I went through in the house. "What happens in the house, stays in the house," she would say. She told me that if I ever told anyone about the abuse, they would call child services and take me away from my family. I would never see anyone I knew again.

It was because I believed I couldn't reach out to anyone that I thought I had to suffer alone. Every day I had to suffer through my pain wondering why the people in my life treated me so cruelly was a day I could've given up on life and made the choice that I would literally never be able to come back from.

We think about networks solely in terms of how our network is our net worth. We tend to only focus on the monetary gain we can get from connections. Rarely do we remember that our network is a connection of people who are human beings first, and therefore the people we add to our network can help us in more ways than just our career goals.

As you embark on your networking journey, I urge you to consider adding people who can help you in life as well as in business. The keys to the good life are health, wealth, love, and happiness. I recommend you begin with health, finding anyone who can help you get in better physical shape, improve your mental and emotional health, and develop a healthier and more positive attitude towards life. Giving special attention and care to your overall health will help you in more ways than just networking. Then and only then, should you focus on the other three keys to the good life.

Action Steps:

1. Keep in mind that if you want to change your situation, you first have to change yourself. To change yourself effectively, you first have to change your perceptions (frames/lens with which you view the world). **[33]**
2. Keep your motivations close
   - In this chapter, you discovered your "why." Always have your motivations in a place where you'll be able to see them. That way, you'll be able to continue moving forward with your purpose in mind. You should never forget the mission. If you have not yet found ways to make your motivations tangible, do so.
3. Use the chapter information to reframe accordingly.
   - If you've been a taker for most of your networking journey and would now like to network using a collaborative frame, reframe from competitive to collaborative whenever you're networking. By "reframe," I mean that if you catch yourself slipping into your old habit of being the only one winning in the interaction, find a way to help everyone win. Find a way to walk away after haven already given something to the other person.

Step Three

Remember the Basic Rules and Principles

In the previous chapter, we covered the mindsets that will be most helpful to your networking journey. (Be sure to complete the action steps at the end of the previous chapter before continuing to this chapter!)

You may be struggling at this point, but stay focused and stay the course. Keep experimenting with different motivations and discover what works for you. If it helps, keep track of your daily successes on a piece of paper. As you advance throughout the day, log each success. If you exercised, put it as a success. If you learned something new about power dynamics, put it as a success. If you cut someone toxic out of your life, put it as a success. Review your successes before you go to bed and finish your day to remind yourself that you are making progress and moving forward. I've even heard of people writing each individual task or habit on a separate sticky note and crushing it in their hands once they'd completed it. They put it in its own special container or trash bin and after a long day, they can look inside the container to see that they absolutely crushed their day (pun intended).

This chapter is all about the basic networking principles that are most beneficial if you're looking to achieve your goals as well as long-term success. This chapter will contain principles and rules to networking that are helpful to anyone with a more short-term mindset, but is geared more toward those who are looking to develop long-lasting, consistent success.

"In the short run, in an artificial social system such as school, you may be able to get by if you learn how to manipulate the man-made rules, to 'play the game.' In most one-shot or short-lived human interactions, you can get by and make favorable impressions through charm and skill and pretending to be interested in other people's hobbies. You can pick up quick, easy techniques that may work in short-term situations. But secondary traits alone have no permanent worth in long-term relationships."[1]

In other words, you need a strong, clear focus on principles if you want any hope of maintaining long-lasting connections for long-lasting success. Techniques are great, but techniques aren't always the answer because techniques change depending on the situation. Principles are an unchanging reference point you can refer back to whenever you're unsure of what to do, what to say, or how to act.

The principles you will learn about in this chapter are not suggestions rooted in teachings found in religion. The principles in this book are independent of any specific religion, doctrine, or other socio-cultural system from theology. These principles are unwavering aspects of the human condition, firm ingredients to the consciousness that exists in all human beings, regardless of any social conditioning. They are the fundamental principles of human effectiveness concentrated toward the art of networking. It's always good to start with the basics.

The Circle of Influence Rule [2][9]

Always be in charge of your circle of influence by managing it on a consistent basis. We have found ourselves in a world where some men and women in their forties and fifties are going broke, while some teenagers are making six or seven figures. Due to technology, age has become a less relevant factor in success. Today, success is more about who leverages their power and, as we previously discussed, one form of power is information.

If they have something you don't have, chances are it's because they know something you do not yet know. One of the most underrated rules to success that some people think they fully understand

---

[9] Information regarding the Circle of Influence Rule provided by author and entrepreneur Peter Voogd. See Notes section for more.

Remember the Basic Rules and Principles

but really don't (or do know about but don't apply) is to keep your circle of influence in check.

Young professionals will look to older adults for guidance because adults have years of experience. If you look to a professional who's older than you for guidance but that particular adult hasn't improved their income or success in twenty years, then they don't have those twenty years of experience. They have one year of experience repeated twenty times. This means that you could get more value, knowledge, and experience (better information) from working with another young professional who's closer to your age that has seen consistent growth and a steady increase in success.

Screen the people in your social circle using your goals. Your circle of influence is the most important key to your success in life and in business. These are the three pieces to your circle of influence:

1.) Support

This category is for family, friends, and the people you hold day-to-day interactions with.

Who is in your support system? The people you keep in your social circle on a regular basis will make or break your ability to achieve your goals. How many millionaires do you talk to on a daily basis?

Bestselling author and entrepreneur Peter Voogd said, "If you want to become a millionaire, talk to billionaires. You'll get there quicker."

I grew up with people who said, "Yeah, but I have my whole life to make money." I grew up with people who delayed building their wealth and focused more on partying. Any money they did have they either flaunted it or spent it on expensive clothes and video games. This social circle wasn't the best motivator for me to stay on track, achieving my goals, so, I cut out the people who didn't align with my vision for the future and for myself.

As your vision gets bigger, this circle should get smaller.

2.) Peers

These are the people you work with. Who do you bounce ideas off of at work? You need what is called a "mastermind network."

These are the people you brainstorm with and exchange ideas with. Ideally, your peers should be people you would trade places with in terms of lifestyle. These are the people who have wisdom and information that can help you get to where you're trying to go. You discover more about your goals and the best ways to reach them through a "mastermind session" with them.

Imagine having a billionaire in your network. Now, your peers don't necessarily need to be that high-power, but that's where you realize that you're really only one connection away from achieving your dream lifestyle. If you want someone like that in your network, you want them as a peer.

This piece to the circle of influence is built around the concept that if you hang around five millionaires every day, you're eventually going to be the sixth. Keep that in mind when evaluating your peers.

3.) Mentor

Who can you learn from that you would trade places with in terms of success and lifestyle that can also cut your learning curve in half?

You're not just learning from how this person gained their success; you're learning from this person's failures so you don't repeat them and take longer to get to where you want to go. Learning from your own mistakes is good, but can be costly and time consuming. Learning from your own past mistakes and the mistakes of others who have already reached the end of the road you're on can help you save time, which is how your learning curve is shortened.

Mentors give you education, guidance, and will call you out when necessary (respectfully of course). They will help you think outside the box and expand the box you've been thinking in. The best part of all this is you can be mentored online. With today's technology, there is no need for you to be mentored in person. This means that you can even get more time with your mentor since it's much easier to meet virtually. In today's world, you don't have to schedule around both of your calendars for a block of time in the day that works for the both of you every time you're ready to learn something new from your mentor.

The Immersion vs. Maintenance Rule [3]

"Immersion is the concept of completely engaging in a certain activity for the sake of improving yourself. This is beneficial, because it allows you to focus *all of your resources* on improving a single skill set or facet of your life."[3]

"Maintenance is the concept of doing just enough to "maintain" your current level of proficiency or balance in a certain facet of your life."[3]

As you learned from the Circle of Influence Rule, it's best to manage your social circle, which means periodically evaluating who's good and who's bad for your personal and career goals. As you weed people out, as your vision gets bigger and your circle gets smaller, the urge will be to start networking more frequently to rebuild your social life, since you've gotten rid of so many bad apples (most of whom were people you talked to every day).

The initial feelings of loneliness are normal and the desire to network and build relationships all the time to get rid of those feelings are completely understandable, but be careful. There has to be a balance.

While the power of money is hugely overestimated in terms of how big a factor it plays in your ability to achieve your goals, it's still important. To immerse yourself fully in your job, internship, or whatever you do that makes you money while also immersing yourself in networking constantly would cause burnout.

As an example, if you choose to immerse yourself fully in the work that generates an income for you, working two jobs, working sixty hours a week or whatever the case may be, it's best to keep your current network on maintenance. Follow up with them every now and then and stay in touch.

Let's say you choose to immerse yourself fully in networking. You're spending money on tools to help build your social media profiles, attending networking events, constantly sending cold emails and cold calling people you want to connect with, and so on. At that point, it would be best to put your other work on maintenance.

You have to have both immersion and maintenance if you want any chance of being successful. The man who does not immerse himself in anything can end up a jack of all trades and a master of none. However, the man who immerses himself in two or more things overexerts himself and collapses mentally or physically before he can achieve any goal or accomplishment of significance.

The WIIFT Rule [4][10]

"WIIFT" stands for "What's In It For Them." To understand this, we look to social and power dynamics where we find a term called "the law of social exchange." Put simply, the law of social exchange is the theory that social relations are based on exchanges of value.

The three major byproducts of this law are that:[4]

1. To get what you want, you have to give others what they want
2. The most popular and powerful people are those with the most to give
3. Strong relationships have a balance of give and take (or at least, the people in them must feel they are balanced)

This is how the "fake it 'til you make it" concept works. People can fake being high-power (having lots of money, having lots of followers on social media, etc.). When high-power individuals perceive these types of people (those who are faking) as high-power, they rationalize that they can create a balanced relationship with them as opposed to if they were to create a relationship with someone who is low-power. In a relationship where one is high-power and the other is low-power, the one lower in power typically spends more time taking in the relationship since they have less to give.

Faking can be done ethically and unethically. Those who have actual power—who are actually high-value—but who do not have the traits of a high-quality man are perceived as low-power, and therefore miss out on opportunities for networking and collaboration. The millionaire who dresses and acts like the homeless beggar does not have the same networking advantage as the millionaire who dresses

---

[10] Information regarding WIIFT provided by power dynamics expert Lucio Buffalmano. See Notes section for more.

and acts like a charming billionaire. In that regard, faking can be done ethically and can open doors that would otherwise be closed.

I hope you see now why it's so important to be perceived as high-power for success at networking. As a high-quality man, you can offer value not just in the forms of money or status, but in the forms of information and personality. High-quality men invest in themselves and are almost always learning. They are also emotionally intelligent, which develops their personality into one people want to be around. You can use being a high-quality man to balance out the difference in value between you and the high-power professionals you're networking with.

Here is an example that further illustrates my point. How willing are you to start a conversation with a smelly, homeless drug addict in tattered clothes? That is the extreme example of the law of social exchange with someone who is low-power (at least that's how we perceive them. That same homeless drug addict could be an undercover millionaire and we wouldn't know). The point is, the relationship is off-balance in terms of value—unless you're also a homeless drug addict.

"Collaborative frames without power will be seen as a kind of weakness and people might try to take advantage of you. That's why the goal is not just to collaborate, but to seek fruitful collaboration from a position of strength. You make yourself into someone who can put value on the table of whatever negotiation in life you go through and then seek others who also have plenty to put on that table and who are willing to collaborate and go for win-win."[5]

To further explain, if you were to find yourself in a situation where that same smelly, homeless drug addict is looking to collaborate with you or do a win-win deal, you may look at the deal as more of a win for him than a win for you, since he is so low-power. There are people who will see this "win-win" deal and use it to take advantage of the poor homeless man. They view his willingness to collaborate as a sign of weakness, since he's not in the best position to be negotiating for anything.

Especially when cold emailing or cold calling people (reaching out to people you've never spoken with or met before), it's best to see the interaction as an exchange of value. If you don't, you put yourself at risk of coming across as awkward and even annoying. WIIFT means focusing on the other person's possible wants and interests.

Examples of good WIIFT moves:[6]

1. Invite them to lunch or dinner and make it obvious you'd treat them
2. Tell them you'd be happy to pick them up at the airport
3. Propose that you will get them into some cool places or clubs that you have exclusive access to

Common mistakes:[6]

1. **"I wanna pick your brain"** = communicates "I want you to give me your time and sit there and answer all of my questions while I give you nothing."
2. **"Let's have a coffee"** = you usually grab coffee in the morning. Here, you're communicating that, "In the middle of the day, right when you're probably working, let's go out while I ask you a ton of questions. And just in case I decide to pay, it will be cheap for me (that's what your input is probably worth, anyway)"

As you can see, the balance in these last two examples is off in terms of the exchange of value. You're using phrases that highlight what you get out of the relationship, but do not take into consideration their interests or what they might want. It's an unfair exchange and can make you come across as someone who doesn't get how relationships or networking works. High-quality men know power dynamics, so they understand and implement this rule—which is another reason they are typically perceived as high-power and have greater success in networking.

Also bear in mind that high-quality men stick to their values. If you do something that violates their values, such as aiming to create a relationship with them where you're only taking, then you've soured your relationship with that high-quality man regardless of how high-power you are.

Remember the Basic Rules and Principles

High-quality men don't care too much about how high-power you are. High-quality men stick to their idea of right and wrong and use their knowledge of power dynamics to effectively create fairness in their lives. A high-quality man understands that we teach people how to treat us and will choose not to sacrifice his beliefs and morals just because you're rich. That would be the equivalent of teaching you that it's okay to cross his moral boundaries whenever you see fit simply because you have a lot of money. A high-quality man will treat himself well so others will be prompted to also treat him well. If you treat him unfairly, you're asking him to set a precedent that it's okay to disrespect him. A truly high-quality man will make the hard choice and draw a line in the sand.

It's smart to network with high-quality men. If they aren't already high-value, they have all the traits that will lead them to acquire resources and status soon. If you want high-quality men in your network, be sure to keep the relationship fair and in balance.

The Fairness Principle

I hope now, after reading the WIIFT rule, you're starting to realize how much truth there is to Chris Voss's words when he said, "Everything in life is a negotiation."

The Fairness Principle is important not just to the law of social exchange, but to collaborative frames. Use WIIFT to make sure everyone in the interaction walks away from a win-win situation that you helped to create.

"Principles are guidelines for human conduct that are proven to have enduring, permanent value. They're fundamental. They're essentially unarguable because they are self-evident. One way to quickly grasp the self-evident nature of principles is to simply consider the absurdity of attempting to live an effective life based on their opposites."**[7]**

I doubt that anyone seriously believes that networking by taking as much as you possibly can and leaving everyone else with as little as possible is a solid foundation for long-lasting success in life or in business.

The law of social exchange is used to ensure fairness and is not to be confused with the "law of reciprocity." The law of reciprocity states that the more you give the more you will receive, but this is not always the case.

For example, networking expert Bob Littell encourages the concept of the "Irrefutable Law of Referral Reciprocity" which means that the more you refer others, the more you will be referred. However, observation as well as real-world evidence (and my own personal experience) has shown that there are circumstances that cause this "law" to lose its effectiveness.[8]

1. If you're actually still networking within a competitive frame (a taker's mindset), even if you don't realize it, you may be putting some strings attached—I'll scratch your back, but only if you scratch mine. Any time you add conditions to it, it eliminates the feeling of obligation to give on the other person's part.
2. When you network within a collaborative frame, you believe in win-win. This means that at some points you will give so the other side can win. What do you think happens when you give to takers? They take and take and take.
3. When someone makes an introduction for our benefit (and this is especially the case if it's a powerful introduction), we tend to take ownership of that new relationship. As the saying goes, "We often forget the girl who brought us to the dance." For me, I think of this as the equivalent of someone scoring a goal in soccer, the crowd going wild, and everyone forgetting the player who made the pass for that goal to happen.

The Integrity and Honesty Principle

Integrity and honesty. "They create the foundation of trust which is essential to cooperation and long-term personal and interpersonal growth."[9]

Faking it until you make it is sometimes dishonest if it's overdone. Becoming a high-quality man is different from faking it until you make it. High-quality men have all the traits that are the highest predictors of success and pave the way to acquiring resources as well as status. In many ways, they are high-value.

Remember the Basic Rules and Principles

Faking it until you make it dishonestly and with a lack of integrity would be lying about how many followers you have on social media, posting pictures on social media of stacks of money giving the illusion you're rich when in reality you pulled those images from a website, and other actions of that nature that inflate your value dishonestly. These methods of "faking it" may work in the short-term but have serious consequences in the long-term. For long-term success, focus more on networking with integrity and honesty, only "faking it until you make it" ethically.

You can appear higher value than you are to attract bigger fish without dishonesty by leveraging and improving the qualities people usually notice about you upon first impression:

1. Attractiveness/Beauty
2. Style
3. Physical fitness
4. Body language / Nonverbal cues
5. Posture
6. Grooming
7. How you walk and move

With an improvement in each of these categories, people will perceive you as higher value and think to themselves that a relationship with you would be balanced. This leads to higher networking success.

The Service Principle

You'll notice that the majority of these principles are about being less of a networker and more of a human being. You're a human being first and should exhibit the qualities of a human first and foremost, such as being compassionate, thoughtful, and giving.

If you want to build connections with people you have to do just that: connect. One way to connect with others is by giving value to them.

"People will forget what you said, people will forget what you did, but people will never forget how you made them feel." - Maya Angelou

Following the Service Principle means serving. The best way to do that is by giving value that makes others feel good. Congratulate them on their promotion or their birthday. A collaborative relationship is about giving value and building each other up. A competitive relationship contains a lot of value-subtracting behavior, such as bragging, lying about your accomplishments, trying to hog attention, or using others for social climbing. These are things that might make you feel good, but not the other person in the relationship or interaction.

As much as this principle is about serving others, there are definitely times when you should serve yourself. A part of the WIIFT rule is taking into account the other person's interests. It's insensitive and unwise to assume that the other side is interested in digging around the internet and your social media to figure out what you bring to the table. Therefore, a part of following the WIIFT rule is self-promoting in a way that signals to the other side you have value without coming across as a crude narcissist.

When some people follow the Service Principle, they network with a "go-giver" attitude and can make the mistake of giving too much. An example that illustrates this point well is a popular habitude (an image that forms leadership habits and attitudes) used by Dr. Tim Elmore:

"The starving baker spends so much time baking bread for others he forgets to eat and starves himself. It looks noble and is noble to keep giving, giving, giving. But just like I need to lead myself before I lead others, I need to feed myself before I feed others."[10]

There's a difference between selfishness and self-care. Promoting your strengths and areas of value is caring for yourself and your career. If you keep quiet, you risk losing out on valuable opportunities because only open mouths get fed. However, as a general rule, it's best to think of the service principle in terms of serving others, not just serving yourself.

The Growth Principle

The Growth Principle is about accepting learning opportunities, even if those opportunities require you to fail in order to learn. If you're afraid to reach out to that CEO or celebrity but you know you would like to connect with them, do it. Accept that opportunity to learn and grow.

Remember the Basic Rules and Principles

Remember, even if you're a master networker, you're not a networker. First and foremost, you're always a learner. That's who you are. The rest follows closely behind.

It's only when you accept that you're a learner first that you can have the self-esteem to network with an antifragile ego. It all starts with being willing to claim and own your identity as a learner.

You want to call that billionaire? Do it. You're not a networker, you're a learner. That means that no matter what happens, as long as you have the antifragile ego you started building in Chapter 2, as long as you're a learner, you're proud of yourself. You take pride not in making the perfect cold calls, but in having the courage to make those calls even when they're far from perfect.

The Patience Principle

Patience is a virtue. Patience is also an important principle to remember if you want to be successful at networking.

Let's say you sent a text to that girl that you can't seem to get out of your head. Let's also say that you know she read that message but still hasn't responded after fifteen minutes. You decide to be patient. A half an hour goes by with no response.

What do you do? You quadruple-text her. That's right. You text her three more messages.

What do you think happens when she hears her phone going off? What do you think goes through her head when she realizes that all three of those rings were not from the entertaining group chat she's in with her girlfriends, but from you?

"She back-rationalizes that if she hasn't replied so far it's because she didn't like you."[11] Now your chances are next to ruined.

This is close to the same effect that impatience will have while networking. If you send three to four emails out of nervousness or any other reason that doesn't involve a life or death emergency, it will not work in your favor.

Be patient. They'll appreciate it more. The last thing you can expect them to appreciate is an inbox full of "Why didn't you return my call" emails.

Like I said, these principles are about being a human being before a networker. Be a compassionate human being and give them the benefit of the doubt. An example of the right response would be to assume that something came up. The right next action would be to reach out to them at a later date with *one* email, asking if your previous email got lost in their inbox.

As a side note, if they don't respond right away, sometimes that's good. It means they're busy. Anyone who is always available with lots of free time is typically not that high-power. That could be a sign that they would be a taker in the relationship. You can tell who's really worth your time by how busy they are.

The word "busy" has three different categories in it:[11]

1. The first kind of busy is the fake kind of busy. Nobody wants to do business with someone who has a lot of free time on their hands. If you were a potential customer for a business and you were looking to connect with the business owner, that business owner having a lot of free time would indicate that they probably don't have too many customers they're busy taking care of. That might be a bad sign for you. Why don't they have any clients? Why are they always so available? Then, to make up for their lack of clients, they go around telling everyone they're busy and make up fake appointments, so you have to fit into their supposedly "busy schedule." (Fake busy is a tactic that can help you from day one, but you can only do that for so long.)

2. Then there is actual, genuine "busy." When they are really busy versus fake busy, you can feel the difference. You will feel it and see it in how they interact and carry themselves.

---

[11] Information regarding the three different categories of "busy" provided by author and entrepreneur Patrick Bet-David.

Remember the Basic Rules and Principles

3. The third type is when they are *extremely* busy. Say they used to meet with you for an hour and a half, but now they only have thirty minutes. They used to have one assistant; now you notice they have three. They do this so they can focus more on what matters to them. All the other tasks they used to do themselves, they have moved to somebody else below their current position. Their value (power and success) has gone up and, as a result, so has their level of "busy."

In other words, a part of you should want it to be hard to create the relationship with them that you're looking for, because if you manage to do so, you've made the cut. Everyone else who couldn't persevere lost the chance to build that relationship, but you didn't.

If it's too easy to build a relationship with someone because they contact you back right away as if you're the most important thing in their entire schedule, you should be concerned about what their true intentions might be. What causes them to be so invested in building a relationship with you when you've hardly had to put in any effort on your end? Not only is it a sign that they may be low-value and could end up being a taker if their schedule is so free, but if they're not even going to pretend to be busy (or fake busy), what does that say about what they might want?

Avoid getting upset when someone doesn't respond right away. Be glad. It's a sign you're probably networking with someone worth knowing.

Action Steps:

Circle of Influence "Support" Steps:
1. Evaluate your support network. Ascertain whether they build you up or tear you down
    - Do they help you advance toward your goals? Do you walk away from conversations with them feeling emotionally good and capable of doing what you put your mind to, or not?
2. Create a "Make It or Break It" list
    - Make a list of the five people that you feel like you need to keep around regardless of if they make you feel like you're

incapable of achieving your goals. These are the people who might be negative but who you really want to keep in your life. Title this list your "maintenance friends."
- Make another list of the five people in your life who most closely share your vision, your goals, etc. These people are encouraging, supportive, and positive. These people motivate you, help you think bigger, and give you solutions. Title this list your "growth friends." You don't need to know these people personally; they can be people you've only heard of and plan on befriending soon.
3. Lower the time you spend with your Maintenance Friends and increase the time you spend with your Growth friends
    - Right here is tough. Right here is where you need to ask yourself if you're willing to do "Whatever It Takes." This is where the "No Mission Too Difficult, No Sacrifice Too Great, Duty First," motto can help you cope with the sudden change in social life you'll experience if you choose to follow these action steps.
    - Remember, the pillars to the good life are health, wealth, love, and happiness—and health always comes first. It may be dangerous for your mental health to suddenly cut everyone off whom you feel may be holding you back. Gradually and slowly shift your time with your maintenance friends to your growth friends. Avoid making any major or rash decisions out of sudden surges of motivation.

Circle of Influence "Peers" Steps:
1. Evaluate your peers against who you can bounce ideas off of; who gives valuable feedback; who you can share strategies, tips, and tricks with; and who can provide you with accountability and support.
2. Connect more with the peers you feel are an ideal fit for your network.

Circle of Influence "Mentor" Steps:
1. Wait until Step Five, where we go more in depth on the mentor category.

Step Four

Networking Strategies to Connect

If you've gotten this far without giving up, you're amazing and I am impressed with your progress. It's not uncommon to surrender in the face of a daunting mission, so congratulations on continuing your work through all the action steps.

The last chapter was all about setting you up with the best (and most effective) networking rules and principles so you can be most effective when you implement the strategies within this chapter.

"If you want to go fast, go alone. If you want to go far, go with others." - African Proverb

Now we get into the good stuff: strategies to connect with others so you can go farther than you ever thought possible!

1.) Know Your Approach

The first step is to know your approach. As previously explained, for you to have greater success in networking, you need to be perceived as high-power.

For the most part, you can behave one of two ways while networking: dominant or submissive. Both have their perks, but in most networking situations you want to be dominant. Why? Dominance is power measured in terms of strength. People who are high-power want to network with other people who are high-power. That way, there is more opportunity for collaboration where both parties are giving and there is less room for the chance of a "one is giving and one is taking" relationship.

High-power individuals seek out other high-power individuals to network with, in order to make sure the relationship they would be creating is in balance. One way to advertise that you're high-power is by behaving dominantly.

The problem with behaving submissively while networking is that "submissive body language and behavior communicates that we accept the dominance of someone else over the environment and/or over ourselves. In a nutshell, submissive behavior relinquishes control and gives power to others."**[1]**

In other words, if you behave too submissively while interacting with professionals, they'll assume that they have more power than you. That leads to them perceiving you as high-warmth, low-power according to the stereotype content model. That's not the bracket you want to be in.

So, while you should be behaving dominantly while networking, different people display and advertise their power (strength) in different ways, so there are many styles of dominance for you to choose from:

Styles of Dominance[2][12]:

1. Physical Dominance: The Meatheads
    - "Meatheads exert dominance through the (unstated) threat of physical violence. It's not uncommon to find executives and CEOs that present a layer of physical intimidation." However, this style is low-warmth and ineffective for networking.
2. Holier Than Thou: The Smart Alec
    - "Smart alecs leverage knowledge to portray authority. Smart alecs carry themselves with a 'better than you' attitude. They act aloof and use big words, slow speech rate, personal distance and quotes to show off how smart they are. Their strategy for social power is elitism and superiority." I'm sure you can see how smart alecs leverage the stereotype content model by presenting themselves as

---

[12] Information regarding different styles of dominance provided by power dynamics expert Lucio Buffalmano. See Notes section for more.

high-power this way. "Since we respect intellectuals in our society, Smart Alecs also have easier access to the elites of power," hence the elitism and superiority behavior.

3. Masters of the Universe
    - "This style mixes physical aggression and confidence with lots of resources. Masters of The Universe (MTUs) temper their physical aggression with suits and the trappings of more civilized social power. They think of themselves as both smart and strong, and they have the confidence of those who believe that nothing and nobody can stop them." You are likely to run into a couple of these types on your networking journey, because these are the guys who most reliably reach top dog positions in their lines of work. After all, mixing civilized aggression, confidence, and an unrelenting focus on making money is one of the most reliable ways for dominant individuals to get rich—and that's exactly what these guys do.

4. Attention Hoggers: The Jesters
    - "Attention hoggers dominate by having the spotlight always on them. Attention hoggers are high energy, loud, and mischievous. Their weapon of choice to dominate others is social embarrassment. They have the power to play outside the rules and the freedom of embarrassing both themselves and the people around." If you find yourself networking with any celebrities who are comedians, you will typically find that they use this style of dominance, maintaining the spotlight on them as they command the attention of the room with a funny story and possibly making light fun of the people around.

5. Flash and Confidence: The Upcoming Young Gun
    - "Mixes physical threat with attention-grabbing flash. It's a style suited for those who are not yet at the top. It's the style of the new kid on the block. These guys talk loud and big, dress snazzy, aim to the top and always make a big show." If you find yourself networking with rappers who have not yet reached celebrity status or whose music is not yet well known, you may find that this style is common.

They may be wearing flashy jewelry and have little to no reservations when it comes to physically threatening anyone who does not consider them a "real rapper."

6. Flashy Trendsetters: The Dandies
   - "Notoriety is the dandies' power. They feed on people's attention and their reward is their attention. Dandies reward with their presence and punish with their disinterest. They are artists, hipsters, VIPs, dandies, fashion stars, and trend-setters." You're likely to come across these types if you're networking with high-power celebrities.

7. Social Skills Power: The Charmers
   - "Their power is social seduction. This is the prototype of the suave man. It's versatile and adapts to different environments, it's sexually attractive and makes lots of friends without many enemies." There are very few cons to this style of dominance and it is the typical go-to for master networkers.

8. The Charismatic
   - "'Follow me, I know the way.' Charismatic leaders deeply believe in something. They are on a mission, they are going somewhere. And they want you to join them." You're likely to come across a charismatic leader or two on your networking journey if you're networking with high-quality, high-value men.

9. Sexual Power: The Seducers
   - "Seducers use sexual lure and sexual energy to influence others. They are like the charmers, but on steroids. Sexual steroids." This style of dominance is more common than you might think. Remember, dominance is connected to power and power is the measure to which an individual can get what he wants. Seducers use sex as a lure to hook in a big fish—a high-quality or high-value individual. You may notice the use of this style to gain other favors, such as seducers using this style to book modeling gigs. Refrain from using this style as a networking strategy; it can be very costly in the long run, as I'm sure you can imagine.

10. Cold and Distant: The Cold Blooded
    - "Their power is social pressure: they unsettle all other 'normal' people. They could smile at you now, kill you in half an hour and not feel a thing. They don't smile, don't joke, and talk little." This style is very low-warmth and does not make it easy to create friendships. You're likely to have a very hard time networking if you behave like a stereotypical mob boss.
11. Been There, Done That: The Dominant Archetype
    - "They exude the calm and confidence of someone who's been at the top for a long time. With little to prove and long experience behind them, these guys are the ultimate archetypes of dominance. They mix the knowledge of their long experience with the coercive power of their 'goons' and the power of the vast resources they accumulated. They get people to move for them with the smallest gesture while they themselves move little and slowly." If you spend enough time networking with financially successful CEOs, you're bound to come across one or two of these.

There are other styles of dominance not included in this list and yet you may have already seen a style of dominance that you like. The common favorite is the Been There, Done That: The Dominant Archetype (DA) since that would present you to the world as someone who is already at the top. However, using this style of dominance without having earned those stripes is misleading and could leave a bad taste in the mouth of those you connect with who realize that you're not as successful as your attitude led them to believe.

The most common dominance style of master networkers is the Charmer. The other styles have cons that prevent effective relationship building. For example, Masters of the Universes tend to be narcissistic and build their confidence on materialism, while Smart Alecs are unrelatable and many secretly resent them.

2.) Choose Your Method[3][13]

Now that you've chosen your style of dominance (let's say you chose the Charmer), it's time to choose your networking method. Different professionals whom you want to connect with may require different methods.

Networking is about building relationships. Therefore, for explanatory reasons, I'll simplify the concept of each method by defining them in the context of a man (the charming networker) looking to build a relationship with a woman (the target connection).

1. The Flirt
    - This is the most common method used by charmers. This is the man—the charmer—who has a way with words.
2. The Detective
    - This is the charmer who, when he likes a girl, does research to find out everything he possibly can about the girl he likes. He researches all of her interests, passions, and things in this world that she loves. This way, when the time comes for conversation, he already has a lot of information he can use to help build a connection. (These types of networkers are incredibly effective.)
3. The Promoter
    - This method is all about self-promotion. When this charmer sees a girl he is interested in, he befriends all of that girls' friends. He presents himself as an incredible guy to all the friends of the girl he likes. He treats her friends well, takes care of them, and may even go so far as to become friends with the parents of the girl he likes. Now, all of the people in her life who hold the most influence over her are telling her what an amazing guy this charmer is. With that, she decides to give the charmer a chance and the opportunity to build a connection is created.

---

[13] Information regarding networking methods provided by author and entrepreneur Patrick Bet-David. See Notes section for more.

4. The Success
   - This is the charmer who might fit into the high-warmth but low-power bracket and is currently the person no one cares about. He understands that he needs to become higher power to get the girl he likes and decides to be so successful he can't be ignored. He aims to acquire enough power to fit into the high-warmth high-power bracket so he can be the guy everyone wants to be around and get that date with the girl he likes. (This is the charming networker who's so successful, everyone is talking about his success.)
5. The Man
   - This is the charmer who understands that before people see him, they see his reputation. He takes care to consistently create and maintain collaborative relationships with the people in his life by giving value. He may give value in the form of encouragement or compliments, or even in something simple and small such as a smile. He does this consistently, because he understands that there is no value in having an old reputation. His charm loses its power if he's recognized as the guy who used to be good, so he continually renews his reputation by giving value on a regular basis. There are no competitive relationships between him and others that involve value-subtracting behavior such as "I'm better than you" or "I told you so." On top of that, he has a reputation for being amazing with other girls, spiking the curiosity of the girl he likes and getting her to decide to see for herself what he's like. (As said by Mark Pagel in his book *Wired for Culture: Origins of the Human Social Mind*, "A good reputation can be used to buy cooperation from people, even people we have never met.")
6. The Comedian
   - This is the charmer who can make the girl he likes laugh. (This is similar to the Jester style of dominance, but with less competition. By less competition, I mean to say that this networker can make people laugh without having to

embarrass others. By operating this way, he maintains his charming qualities.)

Generally, you'll find yourself using more than one method at a time to connect with someone. An example is mixing the Flirt with the Detective. You may research a celebrity you want to connect with, find their number, and then call them. Upon calling them you use the Flirt method. You have the social skills of a charmer and a way with words that makes the building of the connection feel natural over the phone, allowing you to add them to your network.

3.) Use Networking Strategies According to Your Method

By now, you've gotten a handle on how the best networkers approach networking. It's time to start thinking more in terms of networking strategies that are a bit more actionable for your method of choice.

There are hundreds of networking books out there with hundreds of strategies. Some focus on teaching you how to build your personal brand, which would be using the networking method The Success. You may have seen some that teach how to network as The Flirt but are curated more toward introverts who struggle with social situations.

I believe that every situation is different. Ideally, you should oscillate between different networking methods as the situation calls for it. I have outlined a general strategy that will get you started without confusing you too much with advanced material.

Step 1: Play The Detective

Research your target connection. If you're attending a networking event, research who will be showing up and which of the attendees you want to connect with.

Make a list of names and do a thorough review of all of their social media profiles, making notes on anything you have in common to prepare you for the networking ahead. (What's their favorite book? Who's their favorite sports team? What ethnicity are they?)

Step 2: Connect on a Personal Level

It's good to connect on a personal level with the people you meet, especially if you're networking with high-value or high-quality individuals.

We as human beings each have the capacity to be bad or good, takers or collaborators. Different circumstances and mindsets will determine which side of us is drawn out—the win-win side or the taker side. People who are high-power are typically wary of takers and know that advertising their high-ranking position or revealing other indicators of their high value could unintentionally draw out the "Wow, I wonder what this guy could do for me," side of the people they are talking to. That's one of the consequences of creating a circumstance where you start by connecting on a business level (which is connected to your income) instead of connecting on a personal level (which is connected to your humanity).

Try not to be too quick to talk about work with the people you meet for the first time. It's rude, and a good way to be perceived as a taker looking to quickly assess their value to judge if they are worth talking to. Not a very charming thing to do.

Step 3: Converse to Find Commonalities

This is where playing The Flirt is going to come in handy. Converse with the goal of first finding things in common. You can use The Comedian for this as well, cracking jokes along the way.

I've heard some describe networking by saying, "Every first impression with a potential connection is an audition to be their friend." I completely understand where this statement is coming from. First impressions are fragile and hold sway over whether or not the target connection will be interested in continuing to build a professional relationship with you.

However, I don't entirely agree with this statement. It encourages a mindset where you feel the need to prove yourself to the professional you're looking to connect with (since it's an "audition"). In reality, if you're auditioning, they should be auditioning as well. As a high-quality man, you should be qualifying them as a good candidate to be in your network. If you two don't have anything in common and don't see the world the same way (in the sense that you're a collaborator and they're a taker), there's no sense in connecting with them, even if they want to connect with you.

Finding commonalities helps you to screen your connections, but also helps to shift your target connection into viewing you more like a peer and equal. Psychologically (and logically), we like people who are like us more than we like people who we know we have nothing in common with.

This is formally referred to as the Liking by Association principle of persuasion. "One way that 'liking' works is that we buy more from those we like."[4] In this case, you are persuading your target connection to buy into the idea of building a relationship with you.

Whatever you do, avoid getting hung up on all the differences you come across. This could cause you to miss the common ground you need to pull down the walls preventing you from doing business. Keep asking questions and include some clarifying questions to dig deeper, such as, "Can you tell me more about that?" or "How'd you come to that conclusion?" For example, if someone you're talking to tells you that they recently attended a big yoga event, even if you don't share their passion for yoga, you can say, "Wow, that's interesting. What was your key takeaway?"

On the conversational journey to finding common ground, you can start with the reason you both decided to attend the event at which you met and go from there.

A small word of advice: try not to ask too many "why" questions. In negotiation, the word "why" can make your question come off as accusatory. For example saying, "Why did you do it?" has a more negative undertone than "What caused you to do it?" Experiment with using the word "what" in place of "why."[5]

That means that while networking, instead of saying, "So, why did you decide to come to this event?" you can ask, "So, what brings you to this event?"

Step 4: Learn About Their Passions and Motivations

Continue sticking with either the Flirt or the Comedian for now. It's hard to use the other methods, such as The Success or The Man, at this particular stage in the strategy.

Ask them what they're excited about and learn about their passions. This gives them the opportunity to steer the conversation toward something they really care about and want to talk about. Most everybody prefers to talk about things that are important to him or her[6], and charming people focus on the people around them, not on themselves. "Charming people ask questions, love people, and converse well by talking little about themselves[7]." Even though these charming qualities, such as loving people, can be faked (and have been by some politicians), be sure to ask questions with sincere curiosity and work to develop a genuine love for people.

A good question to ask might be, "What do you like most about your position?" Uncover their motivations, reveal their passions, and be sure to listen attentively to their response. If people don't feel like you're genuinely interested in them when you're asking these questions, they'll start to ask themselves what your true intentions are and whether or not they can trust you. This is because you're acting incongruent. Your questions led them to believe you're interested, but your attitude and behavior led them to believe that you're not. Make sure you're congruent by being a good listener with an authentic curiosity so they will want to trust you.

When looking to discover their motivations, asking the right questions is equally important as when searching for their passions. You can ask questions such as, "When you've worked on a project that you felt really good about, what did you like about it?" Then, you can take the conversation a step further and ask them to teach you a little bit about whatever it was that they mentioned. The idea is to get them to expand on what it was they liked about the project, because it invites them to share their passion with you in more detail and creates more opportunity for connection. By finding their motivations, you can find out what they care about and what's meaningful to them.

For example, if they felt good about a fundraiser for mental illness in children, asking them what they liked most about that project will get them to talk more about what they're passionate about. You can also ask them to teach you more about what most don't know about the effects of mental illness on children. You can dig into these topics that serve as key indicators of something that motivates them.

This will also help you later, when you need to think of ways to give value. Can you make a donation to that person's favorite charity in his name?

Step 5: Become Their Wingman

Let's say you're at a networking event. It can be easy to have walked into that networking event trying to call to mind everything you've learned throughout this book and hope you're doing a good job networking. It can be easy to want to know how well you're doing on your networking journey, but let's now think about others who may be just starting their networking journey. Have you ever thought that maybe there are people in the room who are brand new to networking, or otherwise not so good at it?

I won't go so far as to assume you picked up this book because you're new to networking or are rusty around the edges; maybe you only picked up this book in search of ways to refine your skills.

Regardless, chances are there are people in the room looking to network who aren't exactly sure what they're doing. They may be walking around starting and holding conversations, hoping that with enough talking an opportunity will present itself. This is an opportunity for you to add value to them in a unique way.

As it stands, they are probably trying to rely on The Flirt method without knowing anything about it or how to do it properly. Do them a favor and shift them into The Promoter method.

Remember, The Promoter is all about self-promotion. Introduce yourself to the struggling networker and get to know them. Then, after some work finding things you have in common with them and learning about their passions, go introduce that person to other people at the event that you think he or she should meet. As you introduce that person, shine a light on them by sharing an interesting fact about them.

You're helping to present this person as an incredible businessman, father, bowler, whatever you've learned about them that's interesting and can be used to promote them.

Charming people build other people up, but this is why it's so important to become a high-quality man first. People only feel good being built up by people with value. In other words, if a homeless person walked up to you and told you you're kinda cute, are you going to be flattered and blush uncontrollably? Chances are that's a "no."

This step in the strategy can be used on anyone you meet, regardless of if the person you're introducing is a proficient networker or not. Giving value this way is something people will undoubtedly appreciate, including your target connection you started researching in Step One. It will help build your personal brand as someone who operates in a collaborative frame and not as a taker who only wants to build himself up which would be a competitive frame.

After you've completed this step, grab their contact information.

Step 6: Give Value to Your New Connection

Hopefully, you didn't throw yourself on your hands and knees for that executive's business card. Hopefully, that professional didn't hand you a fake smile and say, "Welp, it was cool meeting you," and then walk off without the exchange of contact info.

Unless you did something crazy to make them change their mind about exchanging contact information (or you both had absolutely nothing in common and they decided that they completely hated your personality), gaining their contact information shouldn't have been too hard. If it was hard, good. You're a learner, so those are the exact experiences you need to improve.

One way to give value to your connection is by giving them power. You're giving them power by being a high-quality man—a person with value—and connecting with them. By then, you're both connections in each other's networks, which helps build up both your resources. Connections fall under resources and resources are power in society.

However, if you think that just being a high-quality man and connecting with them is enough to start asking for favors, then you may have an entitlement mindset. This is the person who has a skewed idea of their worth. This person might actually know their worth, but know their worth a little too well. They ask for favors without giving any tangible value, because they have the mindset of, "Do you know who I am?"

If you don't want to come off like a self-entitled prick, give more than just yourself as a resource. There is power in information, and you can leverage that. You can offer your unique perspective on a problem they are having. This is especially valuable, since sometimes it can be hard for a person to get unfiltered access to on-the-ground perspectives about their problem, organization, website, etc.

This is less about how you give value and more about following the Service Principle by giving, regardless of how big or small the gesture is. If you're attending a networking event or a seminar, you can volunteer to help set up the chairs before the event starts. A small gesture, but enough to follow the Service Principle and enough to initiate a conversation.

Step 6.1: Give Value to Your New Connection Creatively
Now, let's say that you want to connect with an executive. Typically, especially if they're higher up than you, their network is bigger (and possibly higher value) than yours. Therefore, you can't rely on giving value through introductions. The connection you're introducing to the executive likely won't be someone the executive feels like they need to add to their network.

You have to get really creative with how you give value, since you need to give value the target will appreciate enough to want to build a further relationship with you. If you can't give value to your target connection, you can operate as The Promoter and give value to the people in that target connection's social circle that they care about.

So, let's say that you're having trouble finding ways to give value to that forty-five-year-old executive who has been in the game for years and has the kind of massive success that makes it hard for him to find the time to chat with you.

This is where it might be time to switch methods to The Promoter. Can you connect with and give value to his twenty-five-year-old son? Maybe he's pursuing music and you can make an introduction to someone you know in the music industry.

If the person you want to connect with is responding to you, work with them to find ways to give value creatively. Volunteer for charitable causes they support. Join their table at a fundraiser or participate in a walk-a-thon with them.

Step 7: Make Networking Notes on Your New Connection

By now, you should have a good idea of who your connection is and what they're like. Take this time to take detailed notes on their interests, preferences, and any other details you deem necessary.

What is a good follow-up schedule for this contact? Monthly? Quarterly? What is their preferred medium of communication? Email? Phone?

The point is to make sure you don't break rapport with your connection by accidentally calling them at an inappropriate time of night because you accidentally confused the time zone they live in with another connection you're talking with.

This is also where you want to make a small note of any good follow-up topics you can use as a quick excuse to get in touch. For example, you can shoot them a quick email if their favorite football team wins the Super Bowl, or you can congratulate them if their company wins a large contract. This is another testament to the power of information, but can only be taken advantage of if you remember these details. The absolute best way to make sure you don't forget is by taking note of them.

Remember, information is a source of power. Keep your relationships strong by keeping an eye on the big picture. Stay up to date and know what's going on with their company at large. You can follow their company or organization on social media, join their mailing list, and even set up Google Alerts to email you any time their company is in the news. That way, when it's time to deepen your relationship with your target connection you'll know what's going on and be able to add value to the conversation on a business level using the information you've acquired.

Step 8: Work to Create a Big Touchpoint

Small touchpoints are small ways of keeping the relationship alive, such as a quick short and sweet email to stay in touch. Big touchpoints are the actions you take that truly deepen the relationship, such as meeting face to face for lunch.

When working your way toward creating that big touchpoint, you should be focusing on giving value so that when you field your request to meet up, it doesn't seem like you're taking their time, their energy, etc. The idea is that since you've already given so much, a meeting is a fair ask.

A great way to give value that builds your progress toward that big touchpoint is sending them a bottle of their favorite wine and then sending them a short video message letting them know you're grateful for their connection and that their willingness to respond to your emails gives you the encouragement to continue working towards your goals. Bring the video to a close with something like, "So enjoy this bottle of wine on me," coupled with a warm smile and boom. A kind gesture like that, asking for nothing in return, is guaranteed to help deepen your relationship to where you feel more comfortable advancing towards bigger touch points without feeling like you're asking for too much too early.

Relationship building is a gradual process. Forcing a friendship is a losing networking strategy. Instead of sending a few small touchpoints like emails and then jumping to a big touchpoint like a business dinner, go from small touchpoints to a medium touchpoint. What I recommend as a good medium touchpoint is asking for a ten- to fifteen-minute phone call—something almost anyone can fit into their schedule.

Make sure that, when making this ask, you make it easy for your target connection to say yes. Communicate why you want to meet them with a good reason. Leverage the persuasive power of "because." In negotiation, I refer to this as preparing your persuasive motive.

You're a seller. You're selling the idea of why your target connection should agree to a ten- to fifteen-minute phone call with you. It is not really a problem to reveal your motives for selling. However, depending on the reason you give, your target connection will be persuaded into a positive or negative reaction.

If you were selling an old phone that you don't use anymore and a potential buyer asked you why you're selling it, what do you think would persuade them to buy? Would your persuasive motive for selling be that the phone is broken so you don't need it anymore? Chances are that would persuade them into a negative reaction and they wouldn't want to buy. Now, if instead your persuasive motive was that you recently got a phone upgrade and that's why you're selling the one you don't need anymore, that would persuade them into a more positive reaction and they'd be more open to buying.

"Everything in life is a negotiation." If you told your target connection that the reason you want a ten- to fifteen-minute phone call with them is to pick their brain on how you can get rich, they may not be too open to the idea of speaking with you. If, however, you said, "I want to grow as a person and respect you, so I would like to learn more about your leadership journey," that persuasive motive has a higher chance of eliciting a positive reaction and getting you another step closer to that big touchpoint you're working towards.

During the phone call, focus on connecting. Your connection can hear your voice, which makes the interaction feel closer than conversing over email. Get to know them better and, as much as possible, do your best to present yourself as a collaborator, not as a taker. Look for opportunities throughout the phone call where you can add value. If it comes up in the conversation that your connection has a lot on their mind because of work, maybe you know a meditation coach you can refer them to.

This phone call is a great time to ask how you can help your connection reach their goals. You can take some of the time in the phone chat to focus the conversation toward how you can help them, so that when it's time for them to help you (by agreeing to a big touch point, like a lunch meetup), it seems like a fair ask.

At the end of this conversation, go back to periodically staying in touch and giving value. Then, ask for the big touchpoint, schedule it, and confirm the meeting.

Step 9: Ask for Advice

Now you're at that big touchpoint meeting with your target connection. It could be something like a dinner or a lunch meet-up. Whatever the case, it's a more intimate form of contact than the usual emails and phone calls.

The general idea here is to value their perspective. You wouldn't be putting in so much effort to connect with this person if you didn't feel like they could provide you with value or help in some way with your goals, so you want to give them the opportunity to provide you with value by allowing them to give you power. In this case, the power we're looking for is information. Get their advice.

Throughout this conversation, continue building trust, building their likability for your genuine, authentic self, and connecting on a personal level. Even though you're taking advice that relates to your goals, avoid making it all about business. It will break rapport and trust, because it's incongruent to how you've been interacting up to this point.

Step 10: Ask for a Referral

Now you've built a relationship with this person. Throughout the duration of your meeting, you two have spent a decent amount of time exchanging ideas. They have provided you with some great advice and the conversation is drawing to a close.

Before the conversation ends, ask them if they can refer you to two more people who can give you some more advice or clarity on a subject you both discussed.

You're not asking for a job and you're not asking for them to refer you to someone who can give you a job. You're not asking for anything major. You only want some more advice and clarity on your goals and you'd love to be referred to someone they trust to give good advice.

If you've been using this strategy correctly, you've built a professional relationship with this connection that feels like a friendship. Ideally, they should be happy to help you. If your new connection can only refer you to one person, that's good. The point is to be able to connect with more people by using the good name of your connection, so you don't have to endure the hassle of reconnecting with them as a stranger all over again. You want to use this process of asking for referrals from people you already know to eventually build up a rolodex of people you feel trust you, respect you, like you, and want to help you.

Step 11: Rinse and Repeat

Repeat this process until you have a robust network of high-quality and high-value individuals who can all contribute to your career and goal development.

As a quick note, you may not always need a big touchpoint before you can ask for referrals. In some cases (especially if your social and conversational skills are advanced), you can ask for advice during your ten- to fifteen-minute phone call in Step 8.

Whether or not you're able to do this is mostly dependent on how well you've built a relationship with your connection. If you've been following all the steps but by the time you get to the call you can tell that your connection still views you as a stranger, focus on continuing to give value and wait until the big touchpoint.

Networking Tips[14]

1.) Take Care of Your Personal Brand. Be As Presentable As Possible.

Your reputation precedes you, so keep your brand consistent. Your personal brand in person could be that you're a charming, high-quality man who loves introducing people, but if your social media—your online brand—contains pictures of you working Friday nights as a male stripper, I can almost guarantee that problems will arise on your networking journey. That's an extreme example, but if you don't

---

[14] Information regarding networking tips provided by author and entrepreneur Patrick Bet-David. See Notes section for more.

treat your social media like an online business card you may miss out on key opportunities. If you leave your strengths and areas of value out of your online presence, people will meet you in person and realize that you were a hidden gem because your social media didn't reflect how amazing you really are. Had they not taken that leap by deciding to meet with you, you easily could've missed out on that opportunity. Keep your online presence consistent with your personal brand to remain as presentable as possible. An example of one way to do this is by keeping your professional pictures up to date on online platforms geared more towards business (such as LinkedIn).

Everybody has a personal brand. Whether you're a CEO or a college student, everybody has a personal brand, because everyone who's alive has a story. In its most simple terms, your brand is what people say about you when you're not around.

"Think about some of your favorite celebrities, public figures, or athletes. Even if you've never met them in person, whatever you thought about them, that conclusion is a reflection of their personal brand. The same thing happens in business because your personal brand isn't just your name, it's what you're known for."[8]

You can start crafting your personal brand by getting clear on your values and then sticking to them. The best networking values are to serve, to help, and to share. Stick to those values like a high-quality man and, in addition to having a brand as a college student or young professional, you'll have a brand as someone who operates within a collaborative frame: someone who is not a taker. That's a brand that attracts great connections and opportunities.

Also be mindful that your value is attached to your brand. People may know you based on your success or your goals, both of which are strong indicators of your value and help to define your brand.

There's nothing wrong with a part of your brand being that you're wildly ambitious and that you love getting things done or that you love people, but keep tabs on your value and your brand. Your value changes as you gain skills and experience. You can use the improvements in your value as a way of improving your brand so that it will bring you more success.

2.) Be Shameless

Being afraid to self-promote can hurt you in the long run. If you're the one approaching professionals but never give them hints at your value, you're essentially expecting them to put in the work to learn more about you and your achievements. That may work in some cases, but only rarely. The key is to know how to promote yourself in a way that doesn't make you come off as the cocky guy who is unpleasant to be around. In other words, learn how to brag about yourself without bragging about yourself.

Here's an example. Some people understand that when you ask a question you are likely to get asked the same question back. It's an unwritten rule of conversation. So, to self-promote, they will ask, "So where did you go to college?" and when asked back, they will say, "Oh, I went to Harvard."

That's sloppy work right there. Instead, tell your victories through personal stories: "You know, it's interesting, I like the fact that you're a baseball fan because one of my good friends, who I knew when we went to Harvard together, he was also a big baseball fan and I remember when..."[9] That's right. You were subtle about it and kept going down the conversational path you were on, as if you didn't just name-drop an Ivy League school.

Now, I don't think I should have to mention this last part, but I've seen it done before. Don't name-drop celebrities you've never met or don't really know as a way of self-promoting. Don't say you met a famous singer when really you were in the stands of a concert with forty thousand other people.

3.) Be Seen

Make sure you're constantly seen. Comment on social media posts, go to the big events in your industry that everyone attends, always be sure to remain relevant in the lives of others.

The "mere exposure effect" says that simply being exposed multiple times to someone leads us to like that person more.[10] When people see you repeatedly, that's how they get closer to deciding to connect with you (and, eventually, making introductions for you). After all, if you were to notice the same woman at every networking event you go to, eventually you're going to wonder who that woman is. You may even decide to spark a conversation with her, solely to figure out who she is. That's the mere exposure effect.

4.) Follow the "Serve Others" Principle. Be Extremely Helpful.

If you spend your time asking without giving, you become obnoxious and annoying and are no longer a charmer. That means you've lost a large part of what made you an effective networker. Be of service to others. Give. Be extremely helpful.

5.) Be Warm and Be Positive.

Even when sending emails, make sure they have a warm tone. Do your best to use positive sentence structure as often as possible while networking.**[11]**

I once had a meeting that kept getting pushed back because the assistant of the person I was trying to connect with wasn't updating the calendar. After the third time, the meeting having been pushed back three weeks now, I reached out with my second email using "positive sentence structure." Here is an example of what I sent:

"Hi Barbara, please adjust your system's calendar to be more coordinated with John's and you will help us avoid the confusion caused by scheduling mix-ups. Thanks!"

Negative sentence structure would have been, "Hi Barbara, please do a better job adjusting your system's calendar to be more coordinated with John's. Our meeting has just been pushed back for the third time which is disrespectful to my time due to an unnecessary mixup on your end. Thanks."

6.) Learn the Art of Small Talk.

Follow the Immersion vs. Maintenance Rule in conversation. In other words, if you are both immersed in a deep topic of conversation, staying there for too long could eventually cause uncomfortable tension. Balance deep conversations with lighter topics that help the conversation flow without becoming awkward.

After going small, you can transition back to deep conversation again. A good way to do this is using networking expert Bob Littell's GLP conversation system[15]. When done properly, GLP—Global, Local, Personal—is a process to enrich the conversation by creating meaningful dialogue (as opposed to small talk).

For example, let's say you are having a conversation with an executive named Dan. You say, "Dan, didn't you mention that you're in the music industry? I know a little bit about the music industry, but I'd love to learn more. If you would tell me on a global or international basis, what are the two or three major challenges that the music industry is facing today?" That would be the "Global." Then you say, "Are those the same challenges within your company that keep you up at night?" This covers "Local" and "Personal."**[12]**

7.) Keep Your Listening Skills Sharp.

You can listen with your ears, but you can also listen with your eyes. In other words, pick up on the social cues of the environment and the person you're interacting with to know if you're still being charming.

The person you're talking to could be furthering the conversation, but only to be polite. If their feet are pointed towards the door, they're using closed body language, maybe they're also crossing their arm over their body to check the time, and they are tapping their feet. Make sure you listen to what they are subconsciously communicating. They may be in a hurry, and you should be respectful of that by politely bringing the conversation to a close (unless it's very important that they hear what you have to say).

8.) Be Your Authentic Self.

If you try to use the Comedian method and you know you don't like making jokes, it will make you come off as insincere. Be yourself. If you're The Flirt, be that. Be what is most akin to your current personality, but don't act outside of yourself. Pretending to be something you're not will raise eyebrows (and not in the good way).

---

[15] Information regarding the GLP conversation system provided by networking expert Bob Littell. See Notes section for more.

9.) Periodically Look in the Mirror.[16]

You want people to "refer" you to other possible connections. Keep in mind that a recommendation is different from a referral. A recommendation is like recommending a good movie. "Hey, you should really watch this movie." A referral is where you have skin in the game and, as a result, your name is on the line. You might put skin in the game by writing an email, making an introductory phone call, or doing something that involves risking your good name.

In other words, if I really value my own reputation and I don't feel the confidence to return the favor after you've introduced me to two or three other people, it's time that you look in the mirror. If you're doing everything right and nothing is coming back around, ask yourself what mistakes you may be making that are causing people to perceive you as not being worth the risk that comes with referring you to a good connection. Frankly, people don't see enough in you that they're willing to take that risk.**[13]**

10.) Master Your Technique.

"Everything in life is a negotiation." Right now, you're negotiating with your target connection to get them to build a relationship with you. You need negotiation techniques that get the other side invested in the negotiation. One that I love is "The Relentlessly Pleasant Negotiation Style." In this style of negotiation, you are "soft in style, hard in substance." You have to be relentless in terms of going after what you want (a professional relationship). If they opened your email but didn't respond, follow up. Do not let obstacles like that get in your way. Do not stop following up and reaching out until you receive a clear "no." While this relentless spirit will get you further than anyone who gives up after setbacks, you will also have a higher success rate by negotiating in a friendly, cooperative, and collaborative way. (You will find that aggression is another losing networking strategy.) So, keep sending those emails, keep reaching out, and keep connecting. Sooner or later, you're going to get an opportunity. As the saying

---

[16] Information regarding the "Periodically Look in the Mirror" networking tip provided by networking expert Bob Littell. See Notes section for more.

goes, "If you hang around the barbershop long enough, sooner or later, you are going to get a haircut."

Another good technique is the "The Liking by Association Negotiation Style": As previously explained, we buy more from those we like. We want your target connection to buy into the idea of building a professional relationship with you. Since you have more power in the negotiation, the more you get the other side to invest by being likable, the more they will like the idea of doing a deal with you (building a relationship with you). This is way more effective than if you lie, show a lack of integrity, talk too much, contradict them, or act judgemental.

Networking Best and Worst Practices[17]

WORST Practices for Connecting with New Professionals [14]

Don't:
- Fail to offer an interesting—even compelling—reason why a new contact should be willing to meet with you. Don't assume that an invitation is enough.
- Offer at least two to three dates or times as options for meeting.
- Offer a convenient (for them) restaurant or other possible meeting place suggestion in your communication.
- Think that meeting with you is the most important thing on their plate.
- Become angry or irritated in your follow-up communication if they don't respond immediately (see above bullet point). Also, don't assume the worst. They could be sick, traveling, etc.
- Fail to give appropriate context as to why you are reaching out to someone you don't know. For example: "Mike, we are both friends with Bill Smith, who encouraged me to meet you regarding a new project I am working on. Your insight would be invaluable and I would be grateful if we could meet to discuss the work. I would also like to see if there is anything I can do to help you. Can you meet for lunch near your office any

---

[17] Information regarding Networking Best and Worst Practices provided by author Randy Hain. See Notes section for more.

days over the next few weeks around 12:00 p.m.?" vs "Hey there Mike. I work for ABC Company and would love to grab lunch. When are you available?"
- Fail to be courteous. Don't forget to be grateful. You have one shot at a first impression. Don't blow it!

BEST Practices for Connecting with New Professionals [14]

Do:
- Try to make a "warm" connection. Can someone who knows the both of you make a warm introduction? This can help overcome obstacles and get you inside the door.
- Suggest a brief introductory phone call before pursuing a meeting, if reaching out to a new "cold" connection.
- Your homework. Check LinkedIn and Google for information about them to find what you have in common. For example: "Jim, I looked at your LinkedIn profile and learned that we both went to UGA and worked at Home Depot, although in different divisions. I am interested in meeting people from your organization and sharing some of the ideas my company is exploring in the supply chain. Do you have time next week on Monday, Tuesday, or Friday for coffee near your office at 7:00 a.m.? Isn't there a Panera Bread down the street from you? I would be grateful for your time and I would love to see if there is anything I can do to help you in return. I look forward to hearing from you. Thanks."
- Respect their preferred method of communication, but understand that connecting cannot be done exclusively by email. Follow up your email with a call. The power of personal connections is important in making this work well.
- Try to view all of this through the filter of "doing business with friends." If you see connecting and business development from this perspective, you are much more likely to build a solid relationship with a new contact before doing business together.
- Be flexible without sounding desperate or like you have nothing to do. Here is a correct example: "Susan, I am open most mornings for coffee except Tuesdays and Fridays—the earlier the

better. I am also available for lunch the next three Fridays from 11:30 to 1:00 p.m. Meeting near your office is very easy for me." Notice how, with this approach, we showed flexibility and offered several options, but they were our options.
- Think long and hard about what value you are bringing to this potential new relationship. Instead of focusing on only what you want, make sure you are considering what might be interesting and helpful for them.
- Always be courteous. Always be grateful. Acknowledge to the other person that you know they are investing valuable time in meeting you and it is appreciated. The basics always work, and this is as basic as it gets!
- Be authentic. To quote Oscar Wilde, "Be yourself. Everyone else is already taken."
- Avoid leading questions. Leading questions are questions that are aimed toward getting the other side to answer in a certain way, typically yes or no. Phrasing questions this way closes the opportunity for open discussion. Instead of asking a leading question like, "Are you happy with your results?" Ask an open-ended question such as, "How do you feel about your results?" Also avoid relying too heavily on leading questions when fielding your requests. Instead of saying, "Is there any way we can meet for lunch at…" or "Do you think you'd be open to a ten- to fifteen-minute phone call…" Instead say, "How open would you be to meeting for lunch at…" or "How open are you to a ten- to fifteen-minute phone call…"

Action Steps:[15][18]

1. Get a piece of paper.
2. Set a timer for one minute.
3. Write down as many first names of people you can think of who are well-equipped to help you with your goals.

---

[18] Information regarding action steps provided by networking expert Michael Goldberg. See Notes section for more.

4. When the timer goes off, start networking. Start at the first name at the top of your paper and research what events they attend, find their email, figure out who you know that could introduce you, get information, and get started.

Step Five

Get a Mentor.
Then, Get Another One.

You're getting close to the end of the book. So far, we've covered the importance of becoming a high-quality man (who knows power dynamics), acquiring the right mindsets, and following the networking rules and principles. You've also learned one of the many sound strategies for connecting with contacts who can best help you reach your goals.

So, why are we talking about mentors? As explained in Step Three, you need to be in charge of your circle of influence. Here's what many don't understand about mentors: the official definition of a mentor is, "An experienced and trusted advisor."

When most people think of a mentor, they think about business, whether that be someone you trust helping you get better at that skill you've been trying to master, or someone who is one of the biggest names in mentor history (such as Benjamin Graham mentoring Warren Buffett, or Bill Campbell mentoring Steve Jobs, Larry Page, and Jeff Bezos).

However, many tend to forget that the Starbucks barista who regularly gets you your "fix" is also your mentor. They have experience doing what they do, and they're advising you to continue getting your fix from them.

People want to think of a mentor as a formal, contractual, professional relationship. They think it only "counts" as a mentorship if you meet with your mentor once every couple weeks. People especially view mentors this way in the world of business.

We think the scam artist seminar host flashing cheesy Powerpoint slides of their Lamborghini is just a guru. We don't think that as we absorb the information they give out that they go from being a guru to being a mentor, but they do.

"A mentor is someone that you have access to (be that access online or in person) that you can watch and see how they do things while taking notes that you can implement into your own life"[1]. When we broaden the perspective of what a mentor is in this way, we realize that we have more mentors in our life than we originally thought. That's why it's important to make sure we approve of the people who act as our mentors.

We must be able to identify which of the mentors in our life are "good mentors" so we can evaluate them effectively moving forward (and follow the circle of influence rule to weed out the "bad mentors"). To do that, we must ask ourselves: what makes a good mentor?

Characteristics of a Good Mentor[2][19]

1. They're a guide
    - They're your guide, not your competitor. They shouldn't be acting superior to you.
2. They're humble and experienced
    - They should be humble and experienced in the skill you're looking to learn from them.
3. They help you help yourself
    - A mentorship should not be an opportunity to get your mentor to do things for you. The high achievers of this world do not do things alone, but they do things themselves.
    - A good mentor doesn't pretend to have all the answers (or try to give you all the answers). Being a good mentor is more about asking good questions that help you figure things out for yourself.

---

[19] Information regarding the characteristics of a good mentor provided by Dan Stotz, the Director of Online Executive Education, and senior lecturer Wes Rhea, J.D. See Notes section for more.

4. They are open to questions
    - They don't just answer questions about how to develop a certain skill set you're looking to improve, but will help you explore and learn more about your area of interest.
5. They help you with both the good and the bad aspects of a job
    - There are highs and lows in both life and business. Ideally, your mentor should be someone who can help you extend the life of those highs for as long as possible and help you learn as much as possible from the lows, all while still keeping you grounded in reality. They should be able to show you that the good won't last forever, and the bad isn't nearly as bad as it could be.
6. They help you learn from their mistakes
    - Your mentor should not be someone too egotistical or narcissistic to admit that they have made mistakes. A part of the added benefit of having a solid network is that you can cut your learning curve in half by learning from your mistakes as well as the mistakes of others. You lose a large part of that added benefit if your mentor is unwilling to share their past failures.

I feel that now is a great time to share the sheer beauty of tearing down the strict barriers society uses to constitute a "real mentor." I'll illustrate my point by sharing a mentor who is nontraditional but has still had a massive impact: Robert Kiyosaki, and his personal finance book, *Rich Dad Poor Dad*.

In that book, he uses his personal story of having two fathers, one rich and one poor, to guide you towards a deeper understanding of the importance of assets and the consequences that come with liabilities. He's humble and tells about his own experiences on his journey to acquiring assets throughout the book. Due to the fact that he delivers his teachings through a book, he can empower you with the information you need to take action while still being unable to hold your hand (something a good mentor should not do). He creates a situation where he must help you help yourself. Last, he helps you learn from his mistakes by telling the mistakes that his poor dad made, which resulted in his missed opportunities for financial success.

In many ways, books could be considered mentors and, personally, viewing books this way helps to keep me motivated to read them. I especially love to read books written by authors who are clear experts in their field and who give action steps in their books, since it feels more like a class that way.

The reason why books are not widely considered mentors is because there is a lack of person-to-person interaction which, as you may have noticed, results in some of the characteristics of a good mentor to be missing. It's hard for a book to help you with the good and bad aspects of your job, since everyone's experience in a given job is different. Typically, to give advice like this would require the assessment of what is currently going well and what's going poorly for you in your profession. It is possible for a book to provide you with that advice if it covered every possible negative and positive experience you're able to have in a job, but it would also result in that book being exhaustingly long.

This is another reason why my book is about networking. By mastering the art of networking, you can create that business relationship with your desired mentor, who can then guide you the rest of the way toward success.

Before we can get to that point, we have to start at the beginning: finding a mentor. To illustrate this step-by-step process of finding and getting a mentor, I'll use the example of a twenty-four-year-old, recent college graduate named Brian who is looking to eventually enter the world of entrepreneurship and CEOs.

Step 1: Map Out Your Ideal Career Path

Let's say Brian has read this chapter with you and now he's taking step one. He creates a rough map of his career path and uses it as an outline from where he is to where he wants to be. To save time, I recommend using the form at www.thecleverconnector.com/careermap. Refer to the model worksheet as you complete the following steps.[20]

---

[20] Career Map model worksheet can be downloaded by going to www.thecleverconnector.com/careermap.

Get a Mentor. Then, Get Another One.

Despite being a recent college graduate, let's say that Brian started networking early. Let's say that he follows the motto, "Dig your well before you're thirsty," and built the relationships he needed before he needed them. He graduated with his bachelor's in computer science, and the contacts in his network have let him know that they'd be more than happy to refer him to a great job that would allow him to achieve Step Two in his Steps for Career Progression list. With the referral from his connections, he would be able to start as a technical support executive right away.

Let's also say that Brian doesn't want to jump the gun. He doesn't want to assume that because he has a degree in computer science that he's automatically a dream candidate for employers everywhere in the tech space. Brian wants to prepare himself for the interviews that will be coming up soon, and he wants to make sure that he has what his employers are looking for. So, he does a little online research.

Through that online research, he found out that employers are looking for important qualities such as customer service skills, listening skills, problem-solving skills, speaking skills, and writing skills. However, Brian wants to know how many of these skills are actually required, and which ones are only qualities an employer would like to see. Brian wants to make sure that most of his resume contains information that employers need in an employee, not just information that employers "would like to see" in an employee. (Brian wants to make sure he has the full meat of his resume and is willing to let any other qualities that are good but not necessary be the icing on the cake.)

Brian, on LinkedIn, types "technical support executive" in the search bar and starts reviewing all of the LinkedIn users who currently hold the position he's applying for. He reviews their entire profile, keeping a close eye on their skills, licenses, and certifications.

Step 1: Map Out Your Ideal Career Path
Career Plan Map

Career Path Summary

I will become the CEO of a technology company before I turn 30 years old.

Steps for Career Progression

1. **College Graduate - I AM HERE**
2. Technical Support Executive
3. Subject Matter Expert/Technical Support Coach
4. Manager

Get a Mentor. Then, Get Another One.

5. Team Leader/Assistant Manager
6. Associate Vice President
7. Vice President
8. Director
9. CEO

Areas I Need to Grow In

1. **Speaking skills** because support workers must describe the solutions to computer problems in a way that a nontechnical person can understand.

Materials & Resources I Need for Growth

1.

He puts himself in the shoes of his employer, realizing that they may make the hiring decision even if the applicant doesn't have the specific certifications for the qualities that employers are looking for. For example, Brian keeps in mind that if the applicant didn't take a class in writing (and therefore has no certificate for it) but had experience in journalism the employer would probably hire anyway. With this in mind, Brian checks the experience section of each profile to see if there's any experience they have that he might need.

After covering all his bases, Brian realizes that one of the most important qualities is speaking skills. This is something that Brian knows he needs to work on. Chances are they would hire him with the speaking skills he has now, but even if they did, there's a slim chance he would be able to advance to Step Three in his Steps for Career Progression list, technical support coach, unless he developed this skill anyway. So, as the old saying goes, "There's no time like the present."

Step 2: Seek Out the Right Mentor Who Has Mastered the Skill You Want to Develop

After reaching the conclusion that developing his speaking skills now would help him land the job he was looking for and help him further his career down the line, Brian gets to work on seeking out the right mentor.

Brian goes back to LinkedIn and searches the companies that his contacts plan on referring him to when he's ready. He makes a quick list of everyone in each company that holds the subject matter expert/technical support coach position and starts researching each of them to get a good idea of how proficient they are in speaking skills.

Brian evaluates each mentor candidate based on their skill level in the skill he's looking to develop. He narrows down the list to five.

Step 3: Get Connected to Your Mentor Candidates

Instead of sending all of his mentor candidates messages to connect, he reaches out to his contacts in his network and asks for an email introduction. If there is a technical support coach who made the

Get a Mentor. Then, Get Another One.

list of mentor candidates *and* works in a company that one of his contacts is referring him to, he asks for an email introduction from that contact first.

For three of the mentor candidates, Brian was able to get connected to the key leaders of career growth that he needed through his contacts. This is what we call a "warm introduction." For the remaining two out of the five mentor candidates, he had his work cut out for him. Brian had to introduce himself as a total stranger and decided to do so via email. This is what we call a "cold email," because he didn't have contacts that could give him a warm introduction.

He used the networking strategy in Step Four to craft those emails, starting with doing some research on his mentor candidates. He started with the first mentor candidate and took note of all the areas where he could connect to him personally, everything he had in common with him, and any indication of what that person may be passionate about or motivated by. For example, the first mentor candidate he researched has a social media profile flooded with images of him volunteering at a nonprofit organization that helps kids without fathers, each picture with a wide smile on his face. Brian concluded that this was something he was passionate about and constructed an email that included that passion in the body of the email. He hit on as many points as he could (commonalities, passions, personal connection, motivations, etc.) without letting the email run on too long.

Step 4: Schedule a Meeting with Your Mentor Candidates

Brian then scheduled and confirmed a meeting with each of his mentor candidates. Since he internalized the networking rules and principles and used the networking strategy, tips, and best practices in Step Four, this part wasn't much trouble.

Step 5: Ask Your Mentor Candidates the Right Questions[3][21]

Brian prepared for the meeting by constructing three questions to ask. Each question was made with intention and directed toward

---

[21] Information regarding asking your mentor candidate the right questions provided by author Simon T. Bailey. See Notes section for more.

drawing out as much value as he could get from each mentor candidate's advice. He stayed away from general questions such as, "So what advice would you give me to improve my speaking skills?" and focused on curating more specific questions so he could get specific answers.

His first question was micro-focused, which means it was directed toward his mentor candidate as an individual. His question was, "What are your keys to succeeding in speaking excellence?"

His second question was macro-focused, meaning it was directed more toward a wider, broader perspective from the mentor candidate's company instead of the mentor candidate as an individual. His question was, "How are speaking skills evaluated by the C-Suite and board of directors?"

Brian's final question was specific to his mentor candidate's wisdom and provided a good opportunity to assess whether or not his interviewee had the characteristics of a good mentor. His final question was, "What do you wish someone would've told you when you were starting out in developing your speaking skills? What lessons did you have to learn 'the hard way'?"

Brian knows that if he is unwilling to admit his past failures or shortcomings, then maybe one of the other mentor candidates would be a better fit for his circle of influence.

As each mentor candidate responds, Brian takes detailed notes to review later. As the meeting draws to a close, before they wrap up, Brian asks his mentor candidate if he can be of any assistance. He maintains a collaborative frame, looking for ways to give back after being given so much quality advice.

Step 6: Turn Your Top Mentor Candidate Picks Into Mentors

At the end of each meeting, Brian asks all of his mentor candidates if he can follow up with them in ninety days.

When Brian returns home, he gets to work. Brian has never been a fan of blindly following orders, so he takes all the advice from his notes and measures them against each other to see which ones he should focus on first and which might not be the best advice for him to follow. The same way he would double-check his work in high school and college before submitting it to the teacher, he uses the advice of each mentor candidate to double-check the advice of the other mentor candidates before deciding which advice he should apply to his daily life. This is one of the reasons why it's important to have more than one mentor.

After filtering out the less useful advice, Brian then applies the best advice from his notes to develop his speaking skills.

After ninety days, Brian will follow up with the mentor candidates that he decided were best for him and his goals. All of the mentor candidates that Brian chose to follow up with will have been turned into mentors without them even realizing it. Any mentor candidates who didn't make the cut, Brian keeps a note of them in case he decides that he wants to network and build a deeper relationship with them later.

Step 7: Gratitude, Gratitude, Gratitude

Remember back in Step 3, when Brian reached out to his contacts to see if they could give him a warm introduction to his mentor candidates? Brian was able to get referred to three out of the five mentor candidates. Brian went back and thanked whomever referred him to those three. He also used this as an opportunity to check in and give them updates on what he's learning, a great way of staying connected when he can't think of any ways to give value but still wants an excuse to stay in touch.

It's not easy, but it's that simple. The key is really about knowing what to expect from a mentorship. Internships are formal. Mentorships can happen throughout our daily lives without our even realizing it.

However, if you decide to formalize your mentorship, clarify your expectations and be specific as far as what you want to get out of the mentorship. If you decide to go this route, talk about the mentoring relationship with your mentor. "How often are we going to meet? How long do we want this mentorship to last? Half a year? How do you prefer to take feedback?"**[4]** Should you meet over the phone so as to be as direct as possible, or in an email where you can read the constructive criticism in short gulps and take your time to process those hard pills to swallow? Get specific to get the most out of your formal mentorship.

As a final note, keep in mind that Brian could choose to use his career map to network with any professionals who hold the job he eventually wants. He can network with the managers, vice presidents, directors, and even CEOs of tech companies if he decides to. That's the power of the technology that has created the interconnected world we live in today. This is also the power of networking as a high-quality man.

Action Steps:

1. Go back to Step Three and reread the Circle of Influence Rule. Take the time to internalize the section on Mentors.
2. Follow the strategy laid out in this chapter and start acquiring the mentors you need.
    - "If you need help designing or implementing your plan, seek the advice of a professional career counselor. (But never pay large counseling fees in advance. Pay only by the hour.)"**[5]**
3. Build up a solid network of mentors to help you improve in any and every area that you're lacking in. This network will be referred to as your "board of trusted advisors".

Step Six

Make Your Own Opportunities

You've made it to the final chapter! At the time of this book's writing, studies have shown that Americans read an average of only twelve books per year. Congrats on making this book one of your reads for this year, *and* seeing it through to the very end.

The last chapter was all about mentors and how to acquire them. You must keep in mind that building relationships is not the process of a microwave: it doesn't happen in minutes. It's a long process that is slow-cooked to perfection. Avoid rushing heavily to build relationships with your trusted board of advisors.

For this chapter, I'll be sharing a couple stories of mine to help give inspiration on your networking journey.

After winning my first acting award and getting so many callbacks, I found myself in a room full of producers, directors, talent agencies, managers, and so many other professionals in the entertainment industry who wanted to speak with me. Many of them were based in different parts of America and had a long flight to catch, so they had to leave the event early.

Not knowing who would be leaving first, I did my best to speak to as many professionals who gave me a callback as possible. As I went from one industry professional to the other, some professionals saw me recognized me from my performance, and pulled me aside to chat after realizing they had meant to give me a callback but didn't get the chance. A good problem to have—but the additional professionals who wanted to discuss possibilities slowed me down to the point that I was unable to get to everyone that had originally given me a callback.

The next morning, I emailed every industry professional who was at the event, regardless of if they gave me a callback or not. I figured that if they didn't like my performance, it didn't matter—we could still build a professional relationship and create win-win situations for each other.

A couple months went by. Things died down and I didn't know what to do. I could wait around for another opportunity, but after working so hard for months and then getting so many big wins at once, it almost felt irresponsible to sit on my hands that way. I was offered a movie deal by a casting director for a project shooting in Philadelphia and had a folder full of business cards, contracts, and letters of invitation to meet with agents and managers. To go from taking my well-developed work ethic to fight for a win like that to sitting around waiting for my wins definitely felt lazy. So, I went to Google and typed in something along the lines of, "How to network as an actor."

After about fifteen minutes of scrolling, reading, and more scrolling, I discovered LinkedIn. It was foreign to me. The first time I used it, I typed in "director" in the search box and a load of directors popped up in front of me. I wasn't sure what I was looking at, but I saw a button that looked like an "add as a friend" button (come to find out the button was actually called "Connect," for connecting with professionals).

As soon as I realized this button was actually a way to add professionals as connections, I figured I would connect with as many professionals as possible. Since the button said "connect" I assumed that as soon as you clicked the button you were automatically connected, as the word implied. I didn't know the "connect" button was actually more like a "send a connect request button" and the receiver had to accept said request.

Needless to say, I spent a good three hours excitedly jamming my thumb on the "connect" button on every director, producer, and casting director, scrolling furiously until around eleven o'clock at night.

The next morning, I woke up to fifty-six LinkedIn notifications from different professionals who had accepted my request. My phone buzzed periodically throughout the day to let me know someone else had accepted my request. The buzzing continued for over a week. I now had over 200 connections on LinkedIn. Out of that 200, only about fifteen to twenty of the professionals I connected with actually sent me a message. Realizing I would have to reach out first (I was very new to networking at this time), I constructed a generic "thanks for joining my network" email that went something like this:

"Thank you for joining my network! I am a young actor in the MD area. I see that you have experience working in the entertainment industry. I look forward to a fruitful working relationship with everyone I connect with on LinkedIn. I see every new association as a possibility to make a friend while elevating my work to the next level!

Thank you for your time!
Ali Scarlett"

From a power dynamics and networking point of view, there is a lot wrong with this. We could take the time to pick this apart, but then you'd miss the rest of the story.

For a quick note on what I mean, one problem with this cold introduction is the fact that I said "thank you for joining my network." Leading with "thank you" that way frames the interaction as if I'm the only one that will be benefiting in our professional relationship[1]. It almost completely takes away what could have been a great chance to underline the value that I bring to the table. Had I said something along the lines of "Welcome to my network," I could have avoided the slightly negative reaction that comes with signaling to others that your primary concern is finding what you can get from them. I wouldn't be surprised if the recipients of my "thank you" message were shifted into assuming that I'm a taker because of my poor word choice. The funny part is, hundreds of industry professionals received that message. Not my brightest moment, but I'm a learner.

Almost everyone who received this message didn't bother with the usual formalities you'd experience in face-to-face conversation. The main response was, "What do you want?", making me feel like most of the entertainment industry professionals were mean. Here I was, being nice, using my good manners by saying "thank you," and the few connections who actually responded were acting like I was a waste of their time (at least that's how it felt at the time, without knowing what I do now).

One of the industry professionals who was kind in response to my message was a former producer who was moving into directing. Originally, he seemed to think that I wanted something from him too, and responded by telling me he's not casting for his film at the moment. I had no idea he was casting for a film.

After some conversation, he offered to let me read the synopsis of the story for his movie. I loved the story and communicated how much I enjoyed the concept, but in the same message told him I'm not looking for any favors at the moment. I emphasized that I'm only looking to make another friend in the entertainment industry. I established common ground, telling him what I had in common with him (from what I could tell, reading the synopsis) and his response was:

"You're close by. Would you like to meet up after the holidays in January to discuss the film and some possibilities?"

We set the date and I met up with him at the agreed-upon date and time. At this meeting, he told me that his film was an epic major motion picture with a budget of roughly $120 million. With a compassionate directness, he expressed to me that with a project this size, chances are I wouldn't make the cut as anything bigger than an extra.

We were meeting for the first time so, at that moment, I couldn't understand why he was underestimating me or my acting ability—but that was really my ego talking. I knew he was just trying to be nice, and I understood the situation. We continued to talk about the film until we shifted more into his passions and drives, where we connected more. We wound up talking for about four hours, then he said, "Would you like to audition?"

I said yes and got an exclusive audition, just me and the director. At that audition he told me I was a great actor and embodied the character better than anyone else he had seen audition (he had seen hundreds; he had been casting for over half a year). He gave me the part. Not as an extra, but as a principal role. We went to his office (which was in another location within the same building) where he handed me a huge script and I was given an non-disclosure agreement (NDA) to sign right then and there.

I tell that story to say this: read the title of this chapter. I gave it that title for a reason. There is more opportunity to be created than you could imagine if only you would create the relationships you need with the decision-makers in positions of power. If only you would put in the work needed to get to where you want to go.

There was no time in any day where I couldn't be doing something more to advance my career. Even if the work I put into my career started with working on myself and becoming a high-quality man, that was fine. The point is that I could always be doing something.

You may have read the chapter title and assumed that by making your own opportunities I meant networking your way to opportunities that benefit your career. That was definitely a big part of it, but you're only seeing half the picture.

There's a reason networking has the word "work" in it. What most people don't understand is that networking is more of an opportunity to work on yourself than on anything else. If you can't communicate, can't show empathy, or have a general lack of soft skills, you'll have a very, very hard time succeeding in a way that lasts.

Growing up, I didn't just have negative experiences with my family, friends, school classmates, school teachers, and soccer teammates. I was disrespected often by some of my neighbors. This is not entirely their fault. They were fed misinformation about me and my goals.

They assumed I had no plans for the future and believed the lies they were told that I was not going to amount to anything. I furthered that idea by choosing to lie that I had no idea what I wanted to do in life. Despite being an accomplished actor at this time with numerous connections in the entertainment industry (and an eye for real estate), I would tell them, "I'm still figuring it out."

Why did I do this? I wanted to see for myself how far the stereotype content model went. I had friends that I knew I could never abandon, simply because they had gone broke or dropped out of college. They would be low-power at that point, but I would still be there for them. I had no real family, so I considered my real friends to be family.

Regardless of any fluctuations in their value and power, I would be there. My friends were the only family I really had, so our friendships were always built on more than just money.

My relationships with my neighbors dissolved when they realized I was a grown adult with seemingly no direction, ambition, or goals of any kind and was not in college. There were days when they pretended not to have noticed my presence.

Every time I would get a win in my career that I chose to advertise on my social media, some of them would reach out to me. You would think that, now that my value had gone up, they'd stick around, but as soon as my win became old news they'd shut me out again. I would get another win, post about it, and the cycle would continue.

The only thing that was truly consistent in my life was self-development. I came back from wanting suicide to working on myself to make sure my choice to live was worth it. There was a time when I nearly died of kidney failure and realized how fragile life truly is. Growing up every day seeing my parents living their lives in their forties and then one day, suddenly coming close to my end at sixteen definitely didn't seem right to me. I thought I would live to at least thirty.

It made me realize that tomorrow really is a made-up idea. We never truly see it, because we're living in today, yet we plan our calendars with the expectation that we're going to wake up tomorrow. Having that experience where my tomorrow almost vanished shocked me into hustling every day to build my legacy and fulfill my purpose.

So, I worked on myself. As I improved, people drew nearer to me. My social life slowly began to improve. I was able to identify who was wasting my time and who would be a great fit for my social circle. I weeded out the people who only saw my value, not the human being in me. I kept people around who could help my mental health. I made my own opportunities by first making myself into a man who could create opportunities. It all started with choosing to work on myself, not just my career.

You may be asking: how does this process work? How does working on yourself translate to real, and noticeable improvements in your life and career? Different areas of your life are complementary. As I said before, the pillars to the good life are health, wealth, love, and happiness. My mental health suffered because I let my negative experiences get to me. As a result, I didn't have the desire to work hard and ended up becoming a very cold person. This resulted in people distancing themselves from me, which caused a lack of love in my life. I fell into depression and my happiness suffered. (The funny thing is, back then, my wealth couldn't have declined because I didn't have any money. It broke the bank for me to go to a private high school with rich kids that had rich parents. I was barely getting by.)

To get back on my feet, I had to push people away who were bad for me and my future. I had to say no to things I would've liked to have said yes to. I would come home, and no one would see the good in me, the hard choices I made day in and day out to remain a good person, or my constant struggle to develop. Instead, they saw disappointment. My father told me, "You're a damn waste of my money," and would routinely threaten to pull me out of the private high school. My mother eventually wanted nothing to do with me, putting me out onto the street.

I was making what could be considered "socially impressive," career-worthy wins at that time, but I didn't trust my mother enough to tell her about them after she cancelled my scholarship. Since I kept all of my success a secret, she assumed I was nothing.

Here's the key to this whole story, the primary lesson I want you to take away from this chapter: I blamed myself.

Everything my parents ever said to me, every time I had ever been abandoned, disrespected, or treated unfairly, I took full ownership. To escape the personal pain that came from never getting answers to why my negative experiences happened, I adopted what you might call an "extreme locus of control." I chose to believe that everything is my fault, because that means I can learn and grow from it. I can use those experiences as opportunities to make sure it doesn't happen again or, if it does reoccur, that I handle it much better than I did back when I fell into depression.

Taking my pain and blaming myself for it led to me making my pain an opportunity to grow. Since it was my fault, I could change it.

This was no different from me leaving my textbook at home on accident being my fault. I am able to learn from that and change by preparing my backpack the night before, moving forward.

That life-changing choice and growth in maturity led to me becoming the kind of man that could create career changing opportunities. The change in my mental health and my mindsets—my frames—led to me improving my overall health, which improved my happiness, which improved my relationships, which improved my success.

Now, that doesn't make those experiences any less painful—-and you shouldn't use this extreme locus of control to beat up on yourself. The idea is to know that you're in control of yourself and how you react to situations in the future.

I accept that as bad as my experiences were, they could've much been worse. My mother could've been a drug addict. Most of the abuse that she put me through was her taking her emotional pain over her collapsing marriage out on me. I don't blame her, and I thank God she never became an alcoholic.

My father was raised by physically abusive parents and that was all he knew about parenting. As I got older and after my parents' divorce, he realized he had done all he could to provide for the family financially, but now had no family. He wasn't really around and didn't take the time to get to know me, so there was no bond.

Eventually, I reached out to him. We got closer through my kidney failure because my mother was unwilling to take me to dialysis. Three days a week, it was me and my father. A two-hour drive to the hospital, three hours of me hooked up to a machine that cycled blood as I did homework, and a two-hour drive back.

Eventually, I let him know what I liked about his parenting and what I felt like he could've done better. I told him how, all things considered I'm very proud of him. I could've been antagonistic and held resentment in my heart throughout every car ride, but I instead took responsibility and accepted all that happened.

Make Your Own Opportunities

This is the power of improving your mental health and taking responsibility. I was able to forgive him for his mistakes and forgive myself for not handling my experiences better. Now my dad is my best friend to this very day.

After forgiving him (and myself), we were able to talk about a hell of a lot more of our struggles and actually laugh about it. Looking back, we could remember the long, two-hour drives to my private school in my dad's broken BMW, where the window slid into the door and we had to tape a garbage bag onto the frame in its place. The interior of the door was missing (all the metal and wires were showing) and the door couldn't shut. Throughout the cold winter, I would hold the door shut for the daily two-hour drive to and from my private school. We laughed as we recalled when my father sent the car to a shop to get it fixed. The car repairman "fixed" the door that refused to close by welding the door onto the car. Now the car door wouldn't open.

As we laughed about the days behind us and talked more with each other, I realized I couldn't have asked for a better dad. I only didn't know how amazing my dad was because he wasn't in my life. Before, I didn't know much about him and held resentment in my heart for that. It was only by blaming myself for our distance that I could tell myself, "My dad not being in my life is my fault and I can change that." It was then that I empowered myself with the ability to step up and warmly open up the opportunity for us to reconnect, every car ride of every day.

My final story for you here is an example of my choice to say no to something I would have liked to have said yes to. At my private high school, there were a lot of rich kids, one of whom I was friends with. Our high school campus didn't have a field for sports practice at the time, so the soccer team went to the private high school nearby for training.

This old friend of mine asked if I would do a drop for him, since I was on the soccer team. He would give me a deodorant, I would get it to a girl over at the nearby high school since I had to go there for practice anyway. I would get a cut of the money. If you haven't already figured it out, there were drugs inside the casing of the deodorant stick instead of actual deodorant. I wanted the money, but I said no.

The next week, I went to a restaurant with a mutual friend of ours who is also on my soccer team. When paying for his meal, he opened his wallet and pulled out a wad of hundreds. My financial situation being what it was, I had to ask how he was making so much money. He told me he picked up the same deal I had turned down and was now making good money off of it. One of my mottos was and still is "whatever it takes," but I stick to my values and follow the law regardless of how big the opportunity is. The money wasn't enough to make me break my moral code, and I am determined to never allow it to be.

Get clear on what success is to you. If you ask me, success isn't a million dollars, and it's not even ten million. It's the achievement of "the good life"—health, wealth, love, and happiness. I invested much time, energy, and money into learning the art of networking because having resources—having connections—is a form of power. You just learned how to network, and you can network your way to opportunities to create this life for yourself. You also just learned how to become a high-quality man, and can work on yourself to create this life. Do both, and be willing to endure. Learn to suffer without complaining. Do it for yourself, because you owe it to yourself. No mission too difficult, no sacrifice too great.

Action Steps:

1. Write down ten things you would do with a romantic partner to show that you love them
   - Soak in a hot tub with candles lit? Dinner and a movie? Maybe you have a hobby you enjoy that you would love to do with them such as singing, boxing, or learning a new language.
2. Schedule a day in the week where you can do as many of those things as possible on that day with yourself.
   - Learn to love yourself more. Learn to enjoy your own company. We appreciate the big things in life, like landing that promotion, but it's not often we spend time learning to appreciate the little things in life, like good music on a nice night. Use this action step to do just that.

Next Steps

You've reached the end of the book, but don't let your learning stop here! Remember, information is a form of power, so you need to continue learning on your journey if you want the power you need to achieve your goals.

Here's a way we can continue to work together. As part of your next steps, whenever you're ready, take this thirty-day challenge (it will take no more than twenty minutes each day) to make sure you're staying on track with everything you've learned in this book to grow your power!

This challenge can be downloaded by going to www.thecleverconnector.com/nextsteps. Upon downloading, you'll also receive clear instructions on how to complete each day's new challenge!

EPILOGUE

This Is Not the End. Quite the Opposite.

Dreams are important. If you decide to put a deadline on your dream, then suddenly the dream becomes a goal, which is also important. Goals mobilize our focus toward the actions that force us to improve as individuals and become the kinds of people capable of achieving our dreams. But it all starts with just that: a dream. However, what is possibly more important than dreams (or goals) is having the power to achieve those dreams.

> "All men dream, but not equally. Those who dream by night in the dusty recesses of their minds, wake in the day to find that it was vanity: but the dreamers of the day are dangerous men, for they may act on their dreams with open eyes, to make them possible."
> - T. E. Lawrence

Many of the young people today who hold dreams, goals, and ambition are lacking the power they need to achieve their desired end results. When this happens, they are at risk of losing the motivation needed to keep trying to achieve, because there's another option: the easy way out.

Many teenagers are engaging in counter-productive, self-destructive, or irresponsible behaviors. A 2020 report by the Addiction Center revealed that, "1 in 5 teens have abused prescription medications, according to the Centers for Disease Control and 1 in 3 parents believe there is little they can do to prevent teen drug use despite evidence that shows parental involvement is the strongest factor in prevention."[1]

It's easy for young people to do drugs and engage in improper activities of the like. It's easy for young people who were once dreamers of the day, fighting for their goals, to turn into people who only dream at night. This means that when there are even a few young people who decide to take the hard route toward the achievement of their own personal goals, it's very important that they have access to the tools they need to stay on that positive path, so as to prevent them from falling into the masses of young people who possess no such ambition and make the easy choice.

This brings us to the root of the problem. Almost everyone knows that they need money to get to where they want to go in life, especially since most challenging endeavors and worthy goals aren't cheap to accomplish. However, the younger generation chalks this up to money being the sole resource they need to bridge the gap between them and their goals.

While they're on the right track in terms of acknowledging and showing respect for the importance of money, they recognize it as the only form of power able to bring them success. They start off on the right foot by getting a job, but most young people enter a job asking: "Where do I fit? What do you value in me?"[2] They ask these questions in the hopes that with the answer they'll be able to thrive wherever it is that they believe they fit. They plan on doubling down on what others value in them so they can get that raise, promotion, etc.

That's all good and well, but this leads to them forgetting about the other forms of power they could be using to reach their desired end result. They spend too much time appreciating their hard skills and give less thought to the importance of soft skills as well as other resources. There's a great point by Dr. Tim Elmore, the president of Growing Leaders, on this:

> "In American history, our public school system in our country was founded by a guy named Horace Mann. At least that's what we attribute it to. Horace Mann first called the public school system the normal school because they were designed

This Is Not the End. Quite the Opposite.

to help kids prepare for the norms of society. So I was just with educators yesterday and I said, 'Are we doing that? Can you say what you're doing in the classroom is getting them ready to have a successful career, to lead a good family, to thrive in a community, to make a difference, to change something before you die?' And you know most of the teachers kind of go, 'I don't know."[3]

In other words, our school system has failed to prepare young individuals for the real world. Chances are this isn't news to you, the real question we must answer is in "how" the school system has failed our younger generation. By understanding that, we can take a look at what young people are lacking and, in doing so, provide them with the tools they need but were not given in school.

There are many things that could serve to be taught in school that would be of great use to young people, such as taxes, personal finance, logical and deductive reasoning, and even healthy skepticism. I believe the educators of today are doing their best, but the current educational system we have now often provides the hard skills that employers are looking for on resumes but does not spend nearly enough time developing the soft skills that help people move forward in life. "Success in the classroom is often 75% IQ and 25% EQ, emotional intelligence. You get out into the working world, it's often the other way around, it's 75% EQ. It's your emotional intelligence."[4]

Hard skills such as math, technology, and engineering are important, but if you can't get along with a teammate, you're not very good at communicating with your boss, or your emotional intelligence is low, your lack of these basic skills could cost you your job and ultimately sabotage your career, as well as your personal life. So, all the grades were right on your report card but, unluckily, you weren't able to translate those calculus lessons into a real life situation.

The reason you've been making progress on your goals so slowly is because you're lacking the soft skills needed to go farther faster. As power dynamics expert Lucio Buffalmano put it:

"Tech skills give you job security. People skills give you board seats."**[5]**

The obvious solution is to learn and develop soft skills. "'People skills' are just as important as 'technical skills,' because even in highly technical jobs, you have to work with others. Many outplacement candidates are technical superstars who've been fired. They knew their jobs, but couldn't collaborate or get along with others. Average performers with strong people skills often last longer. It's better to be a 'people person' with average skills than to be an abrasive expert who wins at the expense of others."**[6]**

Skills alone are not enough. Knowledge alone makes you book smart, but applied knowledge will take you further in life than you could imagine.

"Remember, to learn and not to do is really not to learn. To know and not to do is really not to know."**[7]**

Therefore, the next step is to apply those soft skills to your life and daily situations.

Before you can start networking to achieve your goals, you have to start with your why, which is why we spent so much time on it in Chapter Two. You have to know the purpose behind why you're doing what you're doing.

It was hard for me to find my purpose. It took a lot of self-discovery, because I was searching for a meaning in the pain I had endured. I was hoping that the answers behind the reasons for my pain would guide my path. Eventually, I had to accept that there was no real reason why I went through what I did. The hardest part of that was accepting the unfairness of having to grow up too fast. It was not easy going to school surrounded by people who actually got a better childhood than I did and had a family that loved them, but who would still complain about how they hated their parents.

Eventually, I understood something that changed the way I viewed my purpose in the world: you don't ask life what your purpose is; life asks you. Whatever your response, life will agree. If you decide to

This Is Not the End. Quite the Opposite.

make your purpose robbing banks, life won't grow legs and hunt you down to stop you. The only thing I really knew about my pain was that I hated it. I knew that it wasn't fair, and it was only because I grew up too fast that I was able to handle my problems like an adult at such a young age. What about the people who don't have my strength of will that are suffering the same things I went through? What about people who are the same age as I was back then and aren't sure how to handle the pain of the experiences that I already endured? The way I saw it, I could either share what I learned on my long, arduous journey so they can save themselves the time and unnecessary suffering, or leave those people to figure it out for themselves. I chose the first option, and that was one of my biggest motivators for writing this book.

Once you have your purpose—your "why"—you can start networking. But, as explained in Step One, you will have an easier time networking if you are high-value. In its most vulgar definition, being high-value means being successful in society's definition of success (albeit, there is much more to it than that).

Chances are, in today's world, you'd have a hard time finding someone who didn't want to be friends with a powerful celebrity. Even if only for bragging rights, most everyone would be happy to have a powerful friend. They would enjoy having someone successful in their social circle. This is why it's important to work on becoming high-power (high-value): to achieve the highest level of networking success. Not just so you can be that powerful friend that others want to be around, but so when you want to befriend other powerful people they see you as someone who brings enough value to the table to be worth collaborating with. If you don't bring value to the table, they could view you as a taker. One way to be a high-value man is to be a high-quality man.

As explained in the first chapter, sticking to your values is an important trait to be a high-quality man. One of my values used to be "treat others as you would want to be treated." It's about putting yourself in the shoes of others and treating them how you would want to be treated if you were in their position.

I no longer follow this mantra, because I want to be treated with respect—but will only treat others with respect if I deem them worthy of it. This mantra implies that I should give respect to everyone automatically because I would want to be given respect in their position.

For example, if I walk outside and lock eyes with my neighbor, it's only respectful to give a quick wave to acknowledge their existence. If I were in their shoes, I would want them to do the same, giving some sign that they acknowledge my presence. After all, purposely ignoring people that you made eye contact with and know personally is passive aggressive and rude (unless you're joking).

However, if I walk outside and my neighbor begins to spew a series of racial slurs at me, I have no moral obligation to treat him with respect, even though I would want to be respected if I were standing in his shoes. The mantra "treat others as you would want to be treated" advises me to show him respect, since I would want to be treated with respect as a neighbor, but I feel it is illogical to treat a white supremist who tells me, "Hey boy, if we were in the 1800s I'd hang you from this tree in my front yard," the same way I would treat my kind neighbors. (Thankfully, I've never had this issue with a neighbor, but this example serves to illustrate my point.)

If you ask me, this doesn't give me the moral right to disrespect this racist neighbor (cursing them out or throwing racial slurs back), but I have no obligation to treat them with respect by giving them a kind wave as I would my other neighbors. I can simply walk away. Walking away when you notice someone's presence without giving a sign of acknowledgement is rude and not how I would want to be treated, but for this neighbor I make the exception. For me, respect is no longer given. It's earned.

I also used to believe that all motivations had to be noble. It felt strange to say that selfish motivations like wanting that sports car and mansion were okay. However, as I grew, my values changed in this regard as well. I began to understand that the motivations didn't matter—at least not the motivations themselves. What did matter was how you applied your motivations. If you apply your motivations in a positive manner, the motivation goes from being a self-centered source of fuel to a driving force for good. What do I mean?

This Is Not the End. Quite the Opposite.

If a man decided he selfishly wants to be the richest man in the world and is motivated by acquiring as much power as possible, but decides that the way he wants to reach the top is by giving every dollar in his name to charity and expecting karma to help him achieve his goal, I won't stop him. As selfish as his desires may be, his actions are the actions of a selfless man. He has applied his motivation positively.

I've heard some argue, when I claim the pillars to "the good life" are health, wealth, love, and happiness, that I had left out a key component: faith. My reasoning in omitting faith is that faith cannot be a pillar to the good life, because otherwise the good life would lose its ability to effectively remain. Faith is the foundation on which the good life is built, because faith, at its most basic definition, is simply trust.

I used to feed into the idea that to become successful you needed to believe in yourself. The logic behind that reasoning was that if you don't believe you can do something, your chances of being able to do it are slim to none (since there are already enough forces in the world that are against you). The fact that you are also against yourself reduces your chances of achievement so significantly you may as well give up. However, this is where the power of a network also comes into play.

If Brian doesn't believe in his ability to become a millionaire, but he has a mentor who repeatedly guides him to making six figures a month, he can argue with the mentor that he can't become a millionaire and he can argue with himself, but he can't argue with the results. Every month he's building the wealth pillar of the good life. Eventually, with the guidance of his mentor, he becomes a millionaire. You don't need to believe in yourself, but you do need someone who does believe in you. The key to this working is faith.

If Brian didn't trust the process (have faith in the process) and ignored his mentor's instructions to where he only made a few thousand a month, then he would have never been able to reach his desired outcome and the wealth pillar wouldn't have been able to effectively grow strong. This concept of the necessity of faith applies to all aspects of life—and it is why I said if you don't have a growth mindset you shouldn't bother reading this book. If you don't trust the process or your ability to learn, grow, and develop your happiness, health, or any other aspect of your life, then it won't happen. You don't need to believe, but you need to have trust. Without trust—without faith—the whole temple of the good life comes crashing down.

This is the same concept as the man on the bench press who is struggling to complete his set and doesn't believe he can finish strong. With the encouragement of his personal trainer who stands over him, he's able to do what he wasn't sure he could. He trusts his trainer when he says, "You can do it."

Eventually, you should believe in yourself. However, you shouldn't use it as an excuse not to get started or not to work on yourself. You especially shouldn't use it as an excuse not to network your way to success. You have no idea what you're actually capable of until you take the first step. You will need belief for lasting success, even if that belief doesn't start out coming from you.

As a final note, your self-talk is important. Negative self-talk will hold you back. Some will label their negative talk as just "healthy realism," but at that point it's realistic self-talk and not negative self-talk. There's a difference.

Negative self-talk would be telling yourself you should quit. Maybe you should. I believe in quitting, but only if you're quitting something that's holding you back or distracting you from your main objective. If you know that you shouldn't quit, don't tell yourself that you should. That's negative self-talk.

Develop into a high-quality man and use constructive self-talk to help you along the way toward getting what you deserve in life. You don't have to settle for disrespect or abuse, and you certainly don't have to settle for less than the success and respect a high-quality man receives. We all have the ability to work on ourselves. We all have the power to become more than we are today. We all have the power to fight our personal demons. We can all try to turn our pain into something good. We can all climb out of hell.

Acknowledgments

I would like to give acknowledgement in this book to the following people:

Lucio Buffalmano: For being someone I can trust to stick to their values and for teaching me most if not all that I know about power dynamics. You've been a mentor to me in more ways than one.

Jona Xiao: For showing me how powerful networking truly is and getting me started on my journey to becoming a networking expert.

Chandler Bolt: For giving me the tools and resources I needed to make this book possible.

Dillon Barr: For being willing to collaborate with me on this project by working with Chandler Bolt and helping me get this book into the hands of so many people.

Lise Cartwright: For being my coach and mentor when I needed guidance on how to make this book idea a reality.

Elliott Sanders: For being my very first mentor, patient with me three days a week, every week, as I sat hooked up to a dialysis machine and absorbed all of your wisdom.

Jared Beverly: For being the incredible listener that you are from back when I was depressed and needed to vent out my emotions up to today.

Isaac Bynum: For being one of the most ambitious friends in my social circle that believed in me when no one else did and pushed me to achieve more.

THE CLEVER CONNECTOR

Gerald Norgbe: For being the friend I needed in my time of need when my mother locked me out of the house (with my kidney failure medicine still inside) and I had nowhere to go and no certainty if my kidneys would fail again because I had no access to my medicine. You took me in and showed me a deep act of friendship I hadn't experienced in years.

Read More!

Want another book to sink your teeth (eyes?) into? You can grab the complete guide to growing your personal power (the last self-help book you'll ever need) by going to https://thepowermoves.com/downloads/ultimate-power/!

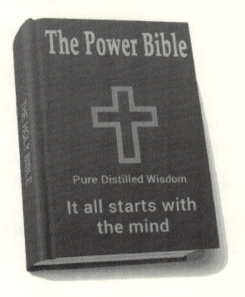

"The only things standing between you and anything you want to accomplish are time and a skillset. The question is, what do you need to learn to achieve it." - Lucio Buffalmano

Notes

INTRODUCTION

1. Dweck, Carol. "Carol Dweck Revisits the 'Growth Mindset'." *Growth Mindset, Revisited* 35, no. 05 (September 23, 2015): 20–24. https://www.edweek.org/ew/articles/2015/09/23/carol-dweck-revisits-the-growth-mindset.html?cmp=cpc-goog-ew-growth mindset&ccid=growthmindset&ccag=growth mindset&cckw=+growth+mindset&cccv=content ad&gclid=Cj0KEQiAnvfDBRCXrabLl6-6t-0BEiQAW4SRUM7nekFnoTxc675qBMSJycFgwERohguZW VmNDcSUg5gaAk3l8P8HAQ.

STEP ONE: KNOW THE POWER DYNAMICS

1. "Stereotype Content Model." Wikipedia. Wikimedia Foundation, February 14, 2020.https://en.wikipedia.org/wiki/Stereotype_content_model.
2. Fiske, Susan T., Amy J. Cuddy, Glick Peter, and Jun Xu. "'A Model of (Often Mixed) Stereotype Content: Competence and Warmth Respectively Follow from Perceived Status and Competition': Correction to Fiske Et Al. (2002)." *Journal of Personality and Social Psychology*, 2019. https://doi.org/10.1037/pspa0000163.
3. Fiske, Susan T., Amy J.c. Cuddy, and Peter Glick. "Universal Dimensions of Social Cognition: Warmth and Competence." *Trends in Cognitive Sciences* 11, no. 2 (2007): 77–83. https://doi.org/10.1016/j.tics.2006.11.005.
4. Buffalmano, Lucio. "Social Skills Overview: Adding Warmth to Increase Power." The Power Moves, May 8, 2020. https://thepowermoves.com/courses/social-power/lessons/warmth-and-power/.

5. Buffalmano, Lucio. "Social Skills Overview: Adding Warmth to Increase Power." The Power Moves, May 8, 2020. https://thepowermoves.com/courses/social-power/lessons/warmth-and-power/.
6. McGraw, Jay. "There Is No Reality, Only Perception." In *Life Strategies for Teens*, 1St Editioned., 141–53. Touchstone, n.d.
7. Buffalmano, Lucio. "The 10 Traits of High-Value Men (W/ Examples)." The Power Moves, May 3, 2020. https://thepowermoves.com/high-quality-men/.
8. "The Science of WHY." Simon Sinek, October 9, 2018. https://simonsinek.com/commit/the-science-of-why/.
9. McGraw, Jay. "You Create Your Own Experience." In *Life Strategies for Teens*, 1St Editioned., 67–83. Touchstone, n.d.
10. Dixon, Walter, and Michael Pantalon. *Instant Influence: How to Get Anyone to Do Anything--Fast*. 1 Editioned. Little, Brown Spark, 2011.

STEP TWO: ADOPT THE HELPFUL MINDSETS

1. Amatenstein, Sherry. "How to Overcome Depression: 5 Things You Can Do NOW to Make a Meaningful Impact." Psycom.net - Mental Health Treatment Resource Since 1986, January 20, 2020. https://www.psycom.net/therapist-plan-for-overcoming-depression/.
2. Buffalmano, Lucio. "10 Frame Control Techniques to Out-Frame Anyone." The Power Moves. Accessed May 30, 2020. https://thepowermoves.com/frame-control/.
3. Covey, Stephen Richards. "Part One, Inside-Out : Paradigms and Principles." In *The 7 Habits of Highly Effective People*, 23–23. Free Press, 1989.
4. Covey, Stephen Richards. "Foreword." In *The 7 Habits of Highly Effective People*, 9–9. Free Press, 1989.
5. MasterClass. MasterClass. Accessed May 16, 2020. https://www.masterclass.com/classes/chris-voss-teaches-the-art-of-negotiation.

Notes

6. Buffalmano, Lucio. "The 4 Fundamental Strategies of Power." The Power Moves, May 23, 2020. https://thepowermoves.com/the-fundamental-strategies-of-power/.
7. Covey, Stephen Richards. "Part One, Inside-Out : Paradigms and Principles." In *The 7 Habits of Highly Effective People*, 21–21. Free Press, 1989.
8. Covey, Stephen Richards. "Part One, Inside-Out : Paradigms and Principles." In *The 7 Habits of Highly Effective People*, 23–23. Free Press, 1989.
9. Covey, Stephen Richards. "Part One, Inside-Out : Paradigms and Principles." In *The 7 Habits of Highly Effective People*, 24–24. Free Press, 1989.
10. Covey, Stephen Richards. "Part One, Inside-Out : Paradigms and Principles." In *The 7 Habits of Highly Effective People*, 28–28. Free Press, 1989.
11. Bet-David, Patrick. "The Evolution of Your Why." Patrick Bet-David, August 24, 2018. https://www.patrickbetdavid.com/evolution-of-your-why/.
12. Dixon, Walter, and Michael Pantalon. *Instant Influence: How to Get Anyone to Do Anything--Fast*. 1 Editioned. Little, Brown Spark, 2011.
13. Taleb, Nassim Nicholas. *Antifragile: Things That Gain from Disorder (Incerto)*. Reprint Editioned. Random House Trade Paperbacks, 2014.
14. Buffalmano, Lucio. "Antifragile Ego - The Source of Eternal, Unassailable Confidence." In *Ultimate Power*, 8–8, 2018.
15. Buffalmano, Lucio. "Antifragile Ego - The Source of Eternal, Unassailable Confidence." In *Ultimate Power*, 8–8, 2018.
16. Buffalmano, Lucio. "Antifragile Ego - The Source of Eternal, Unassailable Confidence." In *Ultimate Power*, 9–9, 2018.
17. Buffalmano, Lucio. "Antifragile Ego - The Source of Eternal, Unassailable Confidence." In *Ultimate Power*, 11–11, 2018.
18. Moore, Robert L., and Douglas Gillette. *King, Warrior, Magician, Lover: Rediscovering the Archetypes of the Mature Masculine*. Reprint Editioned. New York: HarperOne, 1991.

19. Anthony, Jon. "Number Six: Understand Male Psychology." In *7 Strategies to Develop Your Masculinity*, 40–40, 2016.
20. Anthony, Jon. "Number Six: Understand Male Psychology." In *7 Strategies to Develop Your Masculinity*, 42–42, 2016.
21. Anthony, Jon. "Number Six: Understand Male Psychology." In *7 Strategies to Develop Your Masculinity*, 43–43, 2016.
22. Anthony, Jon. "Number Six: Understand Male Psychology." In *7 Strategies to Develop Your Masculinity*, 44–44, 2016.
23. Buffalmano, Lucio. "Antifragile Ego - The Source of Eternal, Unassailable Confidence." In *Ultimate Power*, 10–10, 2018.
24. Bet-David, Patrick. "20 Things That Motivate People." Patrick Bet-David, December 14, 2018. https://www.patrickbetdavid.com/20-things-motivate-people/.
25. Stoltz, Paul Gordon., and Erik Weihenmayer. "Introduction." In *The Adversity Advantage: Turning Everyday Struggles into Everyday Greatness: Updated with New Stories from the Seven Summits and Expedition Photographs*, xx-xx. New York: Simon & Schuster, 2010.
26. Stoltz, Paul Gordon., and Erik Weihenmayer. "Summit Three: Engage Your CORE." In *The Adversity Advantage: Turning Everyday Struggles into Everyday Greatness: Updated with New Stories from the Seven Summits and Expedition Photographs*, 85-91. New York: Simon & Schuster, 2010.
27. Elmore, Tim. "Building A Work Ethic In Today's Professionals." In *Managing the Toughest Generation*, 11–11. Poet Gardener Publishing. Accessed May 11, 2020. https://static1.squarespace.com/static/5b9270fd697a981478cecb71/t/5c5891d09140b749f5a5a2c4/1549308371485/ManagingtheToughestGeneration.pdf.
28. Selig, Meg. "9 Reasons You Need a Personal Motto." Psychology Today, August 21, 2015. https://www.psychologytoday.com/us/blog/changepower/201508/9-reasons-you-need-personal-motto.
29. *12 Military Mottos For Entrepreneurs. Valuetainment*, 2016. https://rb.gy/ecnnxz.

Notes

30. Elmore, Tim. "Building A Work Ethic In Today's Professionals." In *Managing the Toughest Generation*, 25–25. Poet Gardener Publishing. Accessed May 11, 2020. https://static1.squarespace.com/static/5b9270fd697a981478cecb71/t/5c5891d09140b749f5a5a2c4/1549308371485/ManagingtheToughestGeneration.pdf.
31. Mind Tools Content Team. "Pink's Autonomy, Mastery and Purpose Framework: Encouraging Self-Motivation." From MindTools.com. Accessed May 17, 2020. https://www.mindtools.com/pages/article/autonomy-mastery-purpose.htm.
32. Covey, Stephen Richards. "Part One, Inside-Out : Paradigms and Principles." In *The 7 Habits of Highly Effective People*, 28–28. Free Press, 1989.
33. Covey, Stephen Richards. "Part One, Inside-Out : Paradigms and Principles." In *The 7 Habits of Highly Effective People*, 18–18. Free Press, 1989.

STEP THREE: REMEMBER THE BASIC RULES AND PRINCIPLES

1. Covey, Stephen Richards. "Part One, Inside-Out : Paradigms and Principles." In *The 7 Habits of Highly Effective People*, 22–22. Free Press, 1989.
2. *The 6-Step Formula For Building Your "Million Dollar Network" - Overnight. Peter J Voogd*. Gamechangers Inc, 2020. https://rb.gy/dry3ix.
3. Anthony, Jon. "6 Major Life Lessons From Nearly a Decade of Self-Development." Masculine Development, March 3, 2019. https://www.masculinedevelopment.com/6-major-life-lessons/.
4. Buffalmano, Lucio. "Social Exchange Theory: Implications & Examples." The Power Moves, April 4, 2020. https://thepowermoves.com/the-social-exchange-rule/.
5. Buffalmano, Lucio. "Forum, Welcome!: Start Here, Introduce Yourself, Hi, Slightly Confused but Love the Site." The Power Moves, May 22, 2020.

https://thepowermoves.com/forum/topic/hi-slightly-confused-but-love-the-site/#postid-1097.
6. Buffalmano, Lucio. "Forum, Public Forum: Power Dynamics, Case Studies: What's in It for Them Guys, WIIFT, Never Forget It!" The Power Moves, April 5, 2019. https://thepowermoves.com/forum/topic/whats-in-it-for-me-guys-wiifm-never-forget-it/.
7. Covey, Stephen Richards. "Part One, Inside-Out : Paradigms and Principles." In *The 7 Habits of Highly Effective People*, 35–35. Free Press, 1989.
8. Stotz, Dan, and Bob Littell. "Three NetWeaving Mistakes to Avoid." Coursera. Accessed May 25, 2020. https://www.coursera.org/learn/career-advancement/lecture/PYnop?t=79.
9. Covey, Stephen Richards. "Part One, Inside-Out : Paradigms and Principles." In *The 7 Habits of Highly Effective People*, 34–34. Free Press, 1989.
10. Stotz, Dan, and Tim Elmore. "Habitudes for Mid-Career Professionals - Career Habitudes | Coursera." Coursera. Accessed May 19, 2020. https://www.coursera.org/learn/career-advancement/lecture/qArqD?t=103.
11. Buffalmano, Lucio. "What to Text When She Doesn't Text Back (Just Copy Paste This!)." The Power Moves, April 4, 2020. https://thepowermoves.com/7-texts-that-will-make-her-reply/.

STEP FOUR: NETWORKING STRATEGIES TO CONNECT

1. Buffalmano, Lucio. "Submissive Signs: How Submission Looks." The Power Moves, May 8, 2020. https://thepowermoves.com/courses/social-power/lessons/body-language-of-submissiveness/.
2. Buffalmano, Lucio. "Styles of Dominance: Pick Yours." The Power Moves, May 8, 2020. https://thepowermoves.com/courses/social-power/lessons/types-of-dominant-personalities/.

Notes

3. *How to Network Like Casanova. Valuetainment*, 2016. https://rb.gy/hyajmq.
4. Buffalmano, Lucio. "Tai Lopez: Scam or Legit? Persuasion Techniques Revealed - Power Moves." The Power Moves, April 4, 2020. https://thepowermoves.com/tai-lopez-scam/.
5. Buffalmano, Lucio. "Never Split the Difference: Summary & Review in PDF." The Power Moves, April 4, 2020. https://thepowermoves.com/never-split-the-difference/.
6. McGraw, Jay. "You Either Get It, Or You Don't." In *Life Strategies for Teens*, 1St Editioned., 11–65. Touchstone, n.d.
7. Buffalmano, Lucio. "How to Be Charming: The Art of Social Seduction." The Power Moves, April 4, 2020. https://thepowermoves.com/how-to-be-charming/.
8. Bailey, Simon T. "Building Business Relationships - Establish Your Personal Brand." LinkedIn, March 19, 2019. https://www.linkedin.com/learning/building-business-relationships-2/establish-your-personal-brand.
9. Buffalmano, Lucio. "Tai Lopez: Scam or Legit? Persuasion Techniques Revealed - Power Moves." The Power Moves, April 4, 2020. https://thepowermoves.com/tai-lopez-scam/.
10. Buffalmano, Lucio. "Forum, Public Forum: Power Dynamics, Persuasion / Negotiation, Use Positive Sentences: People Focus on Keywords, Not Whole Sentences (Modi Example)." The Power Moves, March 26, 2020. https://thepowermoves.com/forum/topic/use-positive-sentences-people-focus-on-keywords-not-whole-sentences-modi-example/.
11. *How To Self-Promote As An Entrepreneur*. Valuetainment, 2016. https://rb.gy/e3mbud.
12. Stotz, Dan, and Bob Littell. "NetWeaving Skills." Coursera. Accessed May 25, 2020. https://www.coursera.org/learn/career-advancement/lecture/BGXIK?t=119.
13. Stotz, Dan, and Bob Littell. "Three NetWeaving Mistakes to Avoid." Coursera. Accessed May 25, 2020.

https://www.coursera.org/learn/career-advancement/lecture/PYnop?t=79.
14. Hain, Randy. "Best & Worst Practices for Growing Professional Networks." Randy's Blog, April 4, 2014. https://www.coursera.org/learn/career-advancement/supplement/00aOY/best-and-worst-practices-for-growing-professional-networks.
15. *Rediscovering Personal Networking: Michael Goldberg at TEDxMillRiver. TEDx Talks*, 2013. https://rb.gy/xaaet1.

STEP FIVE: GET A MENTOR. THEN, GET ANOTHER ONE.

1. Logsdon, Skyler. "Building Professional Relationships - How Mentorship Works." LinkedIn Learning, December 21, 2018. https://www.linkedin.com/learning/building-professional-relationships/how-mentorship-works.
2. Stotz, Dan, and Wes Rhea. "Finding a Mentor - Finding a Mentor." Coursera. Accessed May 27, 2020. https://www.coursera.org/learn/career-advancement/lecture/7DwF0/finding-a-mentor.
3. Bailey, Simon T. "Building Business Relationships - Find a Mentor." LinkedIn Learning, March 19, 2019. https://www.linkedin.com/learning/building-business-relationships-2/find-a-mentor.
4. Kay, Monica. "Clarifying Expectations of the Mentor Relationship." Coursera. Accessed May 28, 2020. https://www.coursera.org/learn/career-advancement/supplement/cFQpa/clarifying-expectations-of-the-mentor-relationship.
5. Frank, William S. "The Career Advisor25 Hot Tips For Your Career." CareerLab®. Accessed May 30, 2020. http://www.careerlab.com/art_25hottips.htm.

STEP SIX: MAKING YOUR OWN OPPORTUNITIES

1. Buffalmano, Lucio. "Forum, Customers Only: Power University Talks, Re: 'Thank You', When to Use It, and

Notes

When Not?" The Power Moves, December 12, 2019. https://thepowermoves.com/forum/topic/re-thank-you/.

EPILOGUE: THIS IS NOT THE END. QUITE THE OPPOSITE.

1. Juergens, Jeffrey. "Teen Drug Abuse - Signs of Teenage Drug Use." Addiction Center. June 18, 2020. Accessed June 24, 2020. https://www.addictioncenter.com/teenage-drug-abuse/#:~:text=Teen Drug Abuse Statistics&text=1 in 5 teens have,the Centers for Disease Control.&text=Approximately 21 percent of high,National Institute of Drug Abuse.
2. Elmore, Tim. "Building A Work Ethic In Today's Professionals." In *Managing the Toughest Generation*, 22–22. Poet Gardener Publishing. Accessed May 11, 2020. https://static1.squarespace.com/static/5b9270fd697a981478cecb71/t/5c5891d09140b749f5a5a2c4/1549308371485/ManagingtheToughestGeneration.pdf.
3. Stotz, Dan, and Tim Elmore. "Why Are Habitudes Important? - Career Habitudes | Coursera." Coursera. Accessed May 11, 2020. https://www.coursera.org/lecture/career-advancement/why-are-habitudes-important-Ncfh5.
4. Stotz, Dan, and Tim Elmore. "Career Advice from Dr. Tim Elmore." Coursera. Accessed June 1, 2020. https://www.coursera.org/learn/career-advancement/lecture/r87dL?t=26.
5. Buffalmano, Lucio. "Forum, Public Forum: Life Strategies, Workplace Strategies, Tech Skills Give You Job Security. People Skills Give You Board Seats." The Power Moves, April 11, 2020. https://thepowermoves.com/forum/topic/tech-skills-give-you-job-security-people-skills-give-you-board-seats/.
6. Frank, William S. "The Career Advisor25 Hot Tips For Your Career." CareerLab®. Accessed May 30, 2020. http://www.careerlab.com/art_25hottips.htm.
7. Covey, Stephen Richards. "Foreword." In *The 7 Habits of Highly Effective People*, 12–12. Free Press, 1989.

About the Author

Ali Scarlett is an author, speaker, and avid researcher of the art of networking based in Maryland, USA.

His site, www.aliscarlett-author.com, helps young individuals who struggle with the achievement of their goals.

You can get a free Q&A with the author and Career Map template at www.aliscarlett-author.com.

You can also connect with Ali on Instagram @iamaliscarlett and on LinkedIn at Ali Scarlett.

Ali is an actor, his adventures spanning from TV to film. He's an enthusiastic (but terrible) pool player and is the co-owner of a professional cleaning company that has received numerous awards from digital marketplaces. His company connects home and business owners to cleaning professionals. He will also occasionally make a mean Jamaican-style dish.

Ali has studied the work and strategies of multiple networking experts including (but not limited to) Bob Littell, Michael Goldberg, and Dorie Clark. He spent three years in recovery from complications regarding his health before regaining enough strength to dive deeper into the networking world in 2018.

Review Ask

Love this book? Don't forget to leave a review!

Every review matters, and it matters a *lot!*

Head over to Amazon (or wherever you purchased this book) to leave an honest review for us.

We thank you endlessly.

Made in United States
Orlando, FL
06 December 2021